PENGUIN BOOKS

PIANO NOTES

'No one, to my knowledge, is more qualified than Rosen to present the "experience" of playing the piano . . . The great Western classical tradition has had no more persuasive advocate in this century, and his ideas have profoundly transformed the way almost all of us think about the classical repertory' Robert Winter, *New York Review of Books*

'A pleasure to read . . . There should be more musicians like Rosen who are willing and able to write about their experiences with such precision and passion' Angela Hewitt, *The Times Literary Supplement*

'In language of utmost clarity [Rosen] takes you to the heart of the other language of music, not only pulling you to the keyboard, but impelling you to reflect on forms of communication subtler than words' David Hughes, *Spectator*, Books of the Year

'Excellent . . . an important and refreshing addendum to the piano maniac's spiralling collection' Alexander Waugh, *Literary Review*

'For professional pianists of whatever age and experience, this collection of essays is essential reading; its seven chapters should be set texts in every conservatoire; piano teachers from primary school upwards should learn passages . . . the breadth of Rosen's scholarship, the elegance of his prose and the acuity of his observations not only seduced but challenged me into sharpening my critical and listening faculties' Jeremy Nicholas, *BBC Music Magazine*

'A revealing glimpse behind the scenes at the pianistic art . . . Accessible and highly entertaining at all times, the practicing professional and the aspiring student will here find much illumination' Julian Haylock, *Classic FM Magazine*

ABOUT THE AUTHOR

Charles Rosen is a distinguished concert pianist and music critic. He has twice been nominated for the Grammy Award, and his landmark book *The Classical Style* won the National Book Award and has been reissued several times. Its sequel, *The Romantic Generation*, was published in 1996. Today he maintains an active performance schedule around the world, as well as writing for the *New York Review of Books*. He lives in New York City and Paris.

CHARLES ROSEN

PIANO NOTES

THE HIDDEN WORLD
OF THE PIANIST

PENGUIN BOOKS

PENGUIN BOOKS

Published by the Penguin Group
Penguin Books Ltd, 80 Strand, London WC2R 0RL, England
Penguin Group (USA) Inc., 375 Hudson Street, New York, New York 10014, USA
Penguin Books Australia Ltd, 250 Camberwell Road, Camberwell, Victoria 3124, Australia
Penguin Books Canada Ltd, 10 Alcorn Avenue, Toronto, Ontario, Canada M4V 3B2
Penguin Books India (P) Ltd, 11 Community Centre, Panchsheel Park, New Delhi – 110 017, India
Penguin Books (NZ) Ltd, Cnr Rosedale and Airborne Roads, Albany, Auckland, New Zealand
Penguin Books (South Africa) (Pty) Ltd, 24 Sturdee Avenue, Rosebank 2196, South Africa

Penguin Books Ltd, Registered Offices: 80 Strand, London WC2R 0RL, England

www.penguin.com

First published in the United States of America by The Free Press 2002
First published in Great Britain by Allen Lane 2003
Published in Penguin Books 2004
1

Copyright © Charles Rosen, 2002
All rights reserved

The moral right of the author has been asserted

Printed in England by Clays Ltd, St Ives plc

To the memory of Hedwig Kanner
and Moriz Rosenthal

CONTENTS

PRELUDE

THIS IS A BOOK ABOUT the experience of playing the piano. It is not an autobiography, although I have had to draw on some personal anecdotes, but it concerns the experience of playing relevant to all pianists, amateur as well as professional. What has interested me most of all is the relation of the physical act of playing to those aspects of music generally considered more intellectual, spiritual, and emotional, the different ways that body and spirit interact. I have concentrated mostly on professional experience since I know it best, and also because the amateur ideal today is largely derived from the professional standard, but I write for listeners as well as pianists. I have certainly not attempted to tell pianists how they must play. Although my own prejudices have naturally intruded, I have at least tried to keep them under control. There are many valid approaches to the instrument and to its repertoire—and if I occasionally find some approaches invalid, I am not stiff-necked about them, and not wedded permanently to my opinions. I have been most intent on conveying the variety of experience of playing, its torments and its delights.

The temptation is great to write inspirational prose in the grand style about an experience as intense as playing is for any committed pianist. I am embarrassed when I read that kind of prose, however, as the intensity of feeling is only made factitious by being diluted with words, so I have largely preferred to let that intensity be taken for granted. I adore the grand style and I am intrigued by grand synthetic theories, but I am suspicious of teachers who claim to have invented the only successful method for bringing out the best in young performers, of theorists who claim to have invented the unique approach to analysis, and of historians who wish to reduce all the developments of the musical style of the past entirely to the determinism of social conditions. Of course, the place of music in society influences the way we listen and play, but there are so many cases when a composer or pianist produces work badly fitted to the conditions of his or her own time but that turns out for some few contemporaries and then for a later period to be of great value. I have also attempted to discuss the constraints that cause pianists to play in ways to which they are not really committed, and have ventured to speculate briefly on the decisive role the instrument has played in both the history of composition and the reception of music today. Above all, I have tried to become more aware myself of the powerful and peculiar motives that drive some of us to the piano instead of to the violin, the guitar, or the record-player, and of the odd difficulties that this decision creates in our lives.

CHAPTER ONE

BODY AND MIND

ONE OF THE FIRST THINGS a child is taught when learning the piano is to play a C major scale. We always begin with the simple fingering 1 2 3 1 2 3 4 5, and we are shown how to exploit the special character of the human hand and the mobile thumb by crossing the thumb under the third finger as we play the scale; in other scales (E flat for example) we cross the thumb even more awkwardly under the fourth finger. This is a basic part of piano technique as it is conceived in conservatories the world over. Nevertheless, it is a mark of the extraordinary variability of approaches to playing the piano that this fundamental practice is not as useful for some pianists as piano teachers think. A pupil of the late Dinu Lipatti, one of the most interesting pianists of this century, told me that Lipatti once remarked: "You know, it has been at least ten years since I last crossed my thumb under the third finger." I was pleased to hear this, because I too have discovered that this basic position is in fact very uncomfortable. Perhaps that is because my thumb is relatively short, not even reaching up to the middle joint of my second finger. I find that wiggling my thumb into an awkward position moves my hand into an inconvenient angle. It is better for me to keep my hand at a steady angle and displace the arm quickly to the right when shifting from the third finger to the thumb, and I have learned how to accomplish this *legato*. Everything depends, of course, on the shape of the hand, and it must be stressed that there is no type of hand which is more suited to the piano than another. One of the greatest pianists that I ever heard—certainly the most remarkable in his control of the widest possible range and variety of tone color—was Josef Hoffman, who had a hand so small that he could reach no more than an octave; Steinway built him a special piano in which the ivories were slightly narrower so that he could reach a ninth. His friend Sergei Rachmaninov had a very large hand, as did Rudolf Serkin, and Sviatoslav Richter could not only reach a twelfth but could play the last chord of the Schumann Toccata without arpeggiation—an effect which would certainly have astonished the composer. My teacher, Moriz Rosenthal, famous for his technique, had a small hand with stubby fingers; Vladimir Horowitz's fingers were exceptionally long, while Robert Casadesus had fingers so thick that he had trouble fitting them in between the black keys. There is no such thing as an ideal pianist's hand.

In addition, there is no agreement on how to hold the hand at the piano: most children are taught to curve their fingers and place the wrist in a middle position, neither too low nor too high, but of course playing rapid octaves generally demands a higher position for wrist and arm. Horowitz played with his fingers stretched flat and José Iturbi used to hold his wrist below the level of the keyboard.

This variety is the reason that almost all books on how to play the piano are absurd, and that any dogmatic system of teaching technique is pernicious. (Most pianists, in fact, have to work to some extent in late adolescence to undo the effects of their early instruction and find an idiosyncratic method that suits them personally.) Not only the individual shape of the hand counts but even the whole corporal shape. That is why there is no optimum position for sitting at the piano, in spite of what many pedagogues think. Glenn Gould sat close to the floor while Artur Rubinstein was almost standing up. It may seem paradoxical that some pianists spend more time choosing a chair for a concert than an instrument; the piano technician at the Festival Hall in London told me that the late Shura Cherkassky decided on the piano he wanted in five minutes, but spent twenty minutes trying out different stools. The height at which one sits does affect the style of performance. It is difficult, for example, to play bursts of virtuoso octaves *fortissimo* when sitting very low. That is one aspect of piano technique that Glenn Gould, for example, could not deal with (a recording engineer at CBS Records told me that when Glenn recorded Liszt's arrangement of Beethoven's Symphony no. 5, he first played some of the virtuoso octaves in the right hand by using both hands and overdubbed the left hand afterwards); nevertheless, the low seated position enabled Gould to achieve a beautiful technical control of rapid passage-work with different kinds of touch. The way one sits at the keyboard has had an influence on the music that composers write as well as on performance. Ravel also sat very low, for instance, and in his music there are no examples of unison octaves *fortissimo* in both hands which are the trademark of so much nineteenth-century virtuosity, particularly the School of Liszt, and which account for the main excitement in the concertos of Tchaikovsky and Rachmaninov. This Lisztian style of octaves demands a play of the back and shoulder muscles more difficult to manage from a low position. Ravel's *Scarbo,* perhaps the greatest tone-poem for piano of the Liszt tradition, contains no octaves of this kind, but only octaves alternating between the hands, equally difficult to play but not requiring a raised position of the arms.

The famous Lisztian octave passages bring up an important point: the performance of music is not only an art, but a form of sport, rather like tennis or fencing. This is particularly true of piano music, although the violinist who wields his bow aggressively like a sword is not unknown to audiences since the early nineteenth century. The triumphant octave effects are not only the greatest crowd pleasers (when Horowitz was young, members of the audience sometimes stood on their seats to watch him play the octaves in the first and last movements of the Tchaikovsky Concerto in B-flat Minor), they also require special and painful training similar to the hours of exercise to which athletes must submit. Rubinstein, jealous of Horowitz's glamorous success, remarked sardonically to him, "You have won the octave Olympics." It is interesting to note, however, that the most painful of all octave passages to execute are not to be found in Tchaikovsky or Rachmaninov or even in Liszt, not even in the notorious Sixth Hungarian Rhapsody, but in the accompaniment to Schubert's *Erlkönig*. Those octaves obviously gave trouble even during the composer's lifetime when the piano had a much lighter action, since he wrote out a simplified version of this song—simplified for the pianist, that is. It is, however, the brilliant loud octave passages that audiences waited for, just as they wait for the *fouettés* of the Black Swan in the second act of *Swan Lake*, another feat rather more athletic than artistic—although it would be a mistake to deny the dramatic interest of these displays of physical prowess both in piano music and ballet, which have an artistic importance at the very least equivalent to the high altitude arabesques of the mad Lucia.

The true invention of this kind of octave display—or, at least, the first appearance of a long and relentlessly *fortissimo* page of unison octaves in both hands—is to be found in the opening movement of Beethoven's *Emperor* Concerto:

From the opening movement of Beethoven's Emperor *Concerto*

It marks a revolution in keyboard sonority, but it is slower than the rapid virtuoso octaves of the early and late Romantics and not particularly hard to play. It is initially with the generation of composers that followed Beethoven that the performer must experience physical pain with such octaves, starting with Liszt and minor composers like Thalberg. Schumann does not use octaves like that, at least not at a speed to cause the pianist any discomfort except for a brief passage in the *Humoresk* and a much lighter one in the Toccata. Chopin employs such octaves at great length only once and only in the left hand, in the Polonaise in A-flat Major, and he was horrified when he heard a pianist perform them at an unreasonably fast tempo. These famous octaves in the middle section of the Polonaise are popularly thought to represent a cavalry charge, and they are difficult at a rapid speed (one pianist some years ago was rumored to have recorded this piece with her husband playing the left-hand octaves with both hands while she played the right-hand melody).

I have dwelt on this technique, largely outmoded in composition today (the last example that I know in a really fine work is in the final movement of Elliott Carter's piano sonata of 1947, more than half a century ago), not only because of its popularity, but also because hours of practicing parallel octaves have been conjectured to be the reason in recent times for so many pianists' having lost control of the fourth and fifth fingers of their right hand. Bela Bartók in the *Out of Doors* Suite made the effect even more athletic by writing parallel ninths. We have seen in our time the equivalent among pianists of the physical injuries experienced by tennis and football players as a result of their professions.

The sporting element in keyboard performance is already in evidence with the early sonatas of Domenico Scarlatti in the first half of the eighteenth century: here it is the gymnastic aspect of performance rather than physical endurance and strength that played the principal role, with the astonishing leaps of crossing hands and the rapid repeated notes in guitar effects that were Scarlatti's specialty. With the arrival of the so-called first Viennese style of Haydn and Mozart there is a loss of virtuosity: only a few concertos of Mozart and one or two piano trios of Haydn have anything remotely to compare with the virtuoso display that we find in Scarlatti and in Bach's organ toccatas and his *Goldberg* Variations. In the late eighteenth century there was more concern for writing for the amateur rather than the professional in order to sell sheet music, although Mozart was unable to please his publishers and accommodate himself satisfactorily to the demand for easy music. Setting the extraordinary technical difficulty of the music of Domenico Scarlatti and Bach against the keyboard music of the later part of the century, one might think that keyboard technique had deteriorated; in fact, the market for piano music had expanded.

It was Beethoven who felt that the desires of the amateur—or even of the average professional—were not worth attending to, except when he wrote an easy piece to make a little extra money. (Even then, his idea of an easy piece—for example, the first movement of opus 79—was likely to deter the average amateur, just as Mozart composed one of his hardest works—the Sonata in D Major K. 576—under the mistaken impression that he was producing something that could be negotiated by a beginner or an amateur.)

It is important to realize that technical difficulty is often essentially expressive: the sense of difficulty increases the intensity. Composers will write in a detail that sounds difficult but is actually easy to play in order to add sentiment: this is particularly interesting when the difficulty is a mimicry of vocal difficulty— and a great deal of the expression of Western instrumental music is derived from vocal music. Perhaps the most obvious device is the imitation of a singer trying to reach a high note, always an expressive effect. In the Intermezzo in A Major by Brahms, op. 118 no. 2, the leap of a seventh from bar 1 to 2 is made to sound more difficult and therefore more expressive by Brahms through the addition of an arpeggiated tenth:

The opening of Brahms's Intermezzo in A Major

This mimics the difficulty a singer would have. In proofs for one edition of the funeral march in Chopin's Sonata in B-flat Minor, the composer added a grace note which imitates a similar vocal difficulty, and makes the high note more poignant:

From the funeral march in Chopin's Sonata in B-flat Minor

These considerations should be sufficient to show that music is not just sound or even significant sound. Pianists do not devote their lives to their instrument simply because they like music: that would not be enough to justify a dreary existence of stuffy airplanes, uncomfortable hotel rooms, and the hours spent trying to get the local piano technician to adjust the soft pedal. There has to be a genuine love simply of the mechanics and difficulties of playing, a physical need for the contact with the keyboard, a love and a need which may be connected with a love of music but are not by any means totally coincident with it. This inexplicable and almost fetishistic need for physical contact with the combination of metal, wood, and ivory (now more often plastic) that make up the dinosaur that the concert piano has become is, indeed, conveyed to the audience and becomes necessarily part of the music, just as the audience imagines that the graceful and passionate gyrations of the conductor are an essential component of musical significance. This aspect can be abused, we may think: the pianist who looks soulfully at the ceiling to indicate the more spiritual moments of lyricism is a comic figure, and so is the performer who throws his hands into the air to indicate a daredevil recklessness. Both are outdone in unintentional comedy by the pianist who gestures wildly only with his right hand, while his left remains securely planted on the ivories as if he were afraid that he will not easily find its place again. But these are only excesses. For all of us, music is bodily gesture as well as sound, and its primitive connection with dance is never entirely distilled away.

The relation of the performance of music to sound is complex and ambiguous: this is what makes possible Mark Twain's joke that Wagner is better than he sounds. We need to understand the peculiar nature of the production of piano sonority if we are to elucidate the history of music in Europe and America from 1750 to the present. The piano has been the principal tool of composers from that time (less than half a century after its invention) until the present. Piano music is the preeminent field of experimentation.

It has been noted that when Beethoven struck out on a new path, he began with the piano sonata, then turned to the symphony, and consolidated his experiment with the string quartet. The innovations of the early piano sonatas were carried further in the early symphonies; it was not until he was twenty that he published the string quartets, opus 18. The new turn with the three sonatas for piano, opus 31, was followed by orchestral works: the quartets opus 59 confirmed the new style. The piano sonatas opus 106 to opus 111 mark a radical development, and were succeeded by the Ninth Symphony and the Solemn Mass; the last quartets were once again the end of this last change in style. Many composers, in fact, have followed the same procedure. The first decade of Schumann's composing life was devoted almost entirely to piano music. Debussy's first essays at radical harmony are found in his piano pieces. Schoenberg's initial move to atonality is found with his Three Pieces for Piano op. 11; these were followed by the Five Pieces for Orchestra and *Erwartung*. Ten years later, the first dodecaphonic trial is the gavotte from the Suite for piano, op. 25; the Variations for Orchestra came soon after.

Composing at the piano has had a bad press. Berlioz was proud that he could not play the piano, but only the flute, guitar, and tympani: that saved him, he thought, from the terrible influence of keyboard style. The finer composer, it is felt, should be capable of elaborating the work of music solely in his head, and ought not to need the crutch of trying it out at the keyboard. This is an interesting example of the snobbish idealism that wishes to separate body and mind, and considers the body morally inferior to the less material, more ethereal, mind. We have here an ancient aesthetic prejudice: the work of music should be conceived not directly in material sound, but as an abstract form: the realization in sound then oddly becomes secondary. This prejudice against sound has determined a great part of the aesthetics of performance as it is still conceived today. What is considered primary is a set of pitches which we must imagine as independent of any instrumental color: rhythmic indications are less primary (that is, they can be inflected to some extent according to the personal taste of the performer, with rubato and expressive alterations and deformations) but they are still relatively abstract.* Any other

---

* In painting, the corresponding prejudice claims that contour is primary and color is secondary. Ingres, for example, insisted that one could not judge a picture without seeing the engraving.

indications of the composer for dynamics and phrasing may be arbitrarily altered by the performer if he thinks he has a better idea—they are thought to have less to do with the abstract structure of the composition and more to do with the realization in sound. The directions of the composer as to tempo or use of the pedal or fingering are generally treated as simple suggestions that have little or no authority, although both Beethoven and Chopin, for example, indicated the structure of a phrase by fingering, and the pedal indications and metronome marks were often essential to their conceptions. There are very few pianists who pay the slightest attention to Chopin's pedal indications, the majority of editors have disregarded them, and many still today continue to disregard them: they are sometimes infringed or discounted even in the new critical edition that comes out of Warsaw. Almost no pianist, however, would dream of changing the pitch content of one of Beethoven's or Chopin's works (except, of course, when Chopin has provided us with different versions of the same work). The ideas of the composer for the actual realization in sound of his abstract pitches are oddly a secondary matter for most musicians and seem to carry very little authority. The "authenticity" movement has tried to reverse this metaphysical conception, and make the actual sound the composer would have heard or might have heard the primary consideration in an extremely rigid manner. The suppleness of the Western tradition with regard to realization is attacked by the movement (and we have all forgotten the traditionally lax attitude of a good many periods of Western music even with regard to the actual pitch content of a composition, which was much less fixed than we tend to believe).

In spite of the strong moral prejudice against composing at the piano, it has been widely practiced. Haydn always composed at the keyboard. Mozart is traditionally supposed to have composed in his head away from the piano, but in a letter to his father he writes that he is unable to compose at the moment since there is no piano available: "I am now going off to hire a clavier, for until there is one in my room, I cannot live in it, because I have so much to compose and not a minute to be lost [August 1, 1781]."* Shortly after Mozart's death, his biographer, Franz Xaver Niemetschek, wrote about him that "he never touched the piano while writing. When he received the libretto for a vocal composition, he went about for some time, concentrating on it until his imagination was fired. Then he proceeded to *work out his ideas at the piano;* and only then did he sit down and write [my italics]."† In this account we see the prejudice against using the piano while composing, and yet an acknowledgment of its fundamental utility. Beethoven was the great figure who composed away from the piano: that was why his increasing deafness made so little difference to his methods of work. Nevertheless, in his case, his genius at improvising at the piano must have allowed him when young

---

* Quoted from Robert L. Marshall, *Mozart Speaks,* New York, 1991, p. 24.
† Ibid.

to work out many of his ideas directly at the instrument, and this provided him with a repertoire of improvised phrases and motifs that served him for the rest of his life. It is also clear that he hammered out many of his ideas at the instrument for a good part of his life. It was, however, his prestige that made composers after him feel guilty if they were unable to compose without the assistance of the piano. Schumann, in particular, felt ashamed of his reliance on the piano for inspiration.

The utility of the piano for composing was its neutral and uniform tone color: in theory (although not in reality) the tone quality of the bass is the same as the treble. In any case, the change in tone color over the whole range of the piano is, or should be, gradual and continuous (there are breaks, of course, when the notes go from one string in the bass to two and then to three in the treble). The monochrome piano might be used therefore just for its arrangements of pitches, and the quality of the sound could—absurdly in many cases—be considered secondary.

Keyboard instruments are the only ones able to realize and control the entire texture of Western polyphonic music. The use of a keyboard to work out one's compositional inspirations dates from the increasing use of a full score. I do not want to go into the exceedingly complex issue of exactly when composers used a score instead of composing polyphonic vocal music in separate parts, but it is significant that the publication of full scores took a relatively long time to catch on: I presume that composers used scores as a working device to some extent for a considerable time before publication in score became widespread, or even before we have any evidence for it.

In any case, when sophisticated chromatic harmony became fashionable and increasingly sought after in the late Renaissance, the suspicion arose that composers were discovering their effects by accident when strumming a keyboard instrument—a little bit as if "the Lost Chord" of the absent-minded Victorian organist in the once famous poem were found again. The most outlandish chromatic harmonies of the late sixteenth century are in Gesualdo's madrigals, and Alfred Einstein, who claimed that these harmonies induced something like seasickness, thought that Gesualdo must have found these modulations at a keyboard: Einstein seemed to feel that this practice was wicked, perhaps even comparable to Gesualdo's notorious engagement of hired assassins to kill his wife and her lover instead of doing the job honorably himself.

We can find the accusation of composing at the keyboard—which amounts, as I have indicated, to slander, above all when true—much earlier than the twentieth-century musicologist Alfred Einstein's charges. During his lifetime Monteverdi was attacked for the same crime; he was said to have discovered his dissonances at the keyboard. It was thought to be sinful above all to work out vocal harmony at the keyboard, principally because instrumental (above all, keyboard) tuning was different from vocal intonation, and one could not adjust the tuning of the organ in mid-phrase as a singer could inflect the intonation of a note. In his attack on composers like Monteverdi, entitled revealingly *Delle imperfettioni della moderna musica ["Of the Imperfections of Modern Music"]*, the conservative critic Giovanni Maria Artusi in 1600 attacked what he called the harsh dissonances of Monteverdi. They deceive the ear, he claimed:

> *These composers . . seek only to satisfy the ear and with this aim toil night and day at their instruments to hear the effect which passages so made produce; the poor fellows do not perceive that what the instruments tell them is false and that it is one thing to search with voices and instruments for something pertaining to the harmonic faculty, another to arrive at the exact truth by means of reasons seconded by the ear.*

We see here the formation of the prejudice against composition arrived at pragmatically by physically testing the sound instead of mentally planning it by logic, rules, and traditional reason and using the ear only in a secondary role to ratify the results arrived.

It is easy enough to demonstrate that this opposition of body and mind is unrealistic if we consider improvisation. It may not be completely true to say that the fingers of the pianist have a reason of their own that reason knows not of, because improvisation is not exactly unconscious, but it is clear that the fingers develop a partially independent logic which is only ratified by the mind. Perhaps one should add that interpretation, too, works very much like improvisation. In playing a Chopin ballade, an interpretation can be as much an instinctive muscular reaction of the body as a reasoned approach. That is, in fact, one of the problems of interpretation: a tradition of performance is often a mechanical substitute for thought or inspiration, built in physically—often a happy substitute, but it becomes a disastrous inhibition when the tradition has degenerated into a lax and unquestioned reminiscence of earlier performance. The unthinking, unplanned performance—and this is an incontrovertible fact of modern concert life—is generally far less spontaneous, much more the prisoner of habit, than one that questions the traditional point of view, in which the performer questions his own instincts. The musician who has surrendered his will to tradition has abandoned the possibility of keeping the tradition alive.

The greatest interaction between keyboard instrument and the process of composition begins with the invention of the pianoforte, the *Hammerklavier,* in the early eighteenth century. Perhaps the first works written with the knowledge that they would be played on the recent invention are the two ricercares from Bach's *Musical Offering.* The new instrument gradually asserted its supremacy over the harpsichord for use in public halls (there had never been any question of employing the clavichord for this purpose): the organ, ideologically as well as physically tied to the church, lost its dominance with the diminished interest in ecclesiastical music. Even today the organ is irrevocably tainted with religiosity. The importance of the piano was not, however, simply its greater sonority, or even its ability to realize dynamic nuances. It was, I think, above all the fact that it was the only instrument that could both realize an entire musical score on its own and at the same time call into play all the muscular effort of the body of the performer. A loud note on the organ requires no extra effort on the part of the performer, and only a minimal increase on the harpsichord is necessary (coupling the manuals to gain more sonority makes the action slightly more resistant). Trying for a loud sonority on the clavichord only succeeds in knocking it out of tune: it is capable of a most delicate sophistication, and can achieve a lovely vibrato denied to all the other keyboard instruments, but it calls upon very little corporal force, and does not engage the muscles—the body—of the performer. With the piano, every increase of sound is felt by the whole body of the pianist, bringing into play back and shoulder muscles. The performer has to cooperate directly in every crescendo and decrescendo: playing the piano is closer to the origin of music in dance than performing on the earlier keyboards that it superceded. The danger of the piano, and its glory, is that the pianist can feel the music with his whole body without having to listen to it.

With the invention of the piano came the structural use not only of a contrast of dynamics but of a gradual transition from one dynamic level to another. This kind of transition existed, of course, before the second half of the eighteenth century, but it was expressive, not structural—within the interior of the phrase, not as a means of articulating the large form. Only an articulated contrast of dynamic levels played an important role in structure until the 1760s. It is with the gradual *crescendo* over a complete phrase or more that the piano came fully into its own. Later, with the invention of the cast iron frame that made possible the large instruments in the nineteenth century, the athletic element of performance became a basic attraction with what might be called the exhilaration of violence. The exertion needed to produce the greatest fortissimo makes the pianist feel as if merged with the instrument, participating directly in the creation of the volume of sound like a string or wind player. The size of the piano, however, so much greater than violin or flute, induces the belief that one is dominating the sound from within like a singer, as if mastering it were to become part of it; and therefore to a greater extent than any other instrumentalist the pianist enters into the full polyphonic texture of the music.

The intimate relation between physical effort and expression on the piano influences both composition and performance. Composers and pianists feel instinctively that the very movements of hand and arm should be in keeping with the musical conception. In his last published mazurka, Chopin wrote his only canon (a form in which a single melodic line makes harmony with itself by being placed in two voices, one starting a few beats later than the other), and he clearly demands that the pianist play both voices with one hand:

From the canon in Chopin's last published Mazurka, in C-sharp Minor

It is, in fact, awkward to play both voices in the right hand, as no pianist's hand is large enough to play some of the required notes simultaneously, and most editors give a fingering which allows the left hand to help by playing some of the notes of the canon. However, whenever an interval exceeds the compass of the hand, Chopin directs the pianist to arpeggiate. It is evident that he wished not only to hear the canon, but to feel the two-part counterpoint in one hand. The enforced stretch was a part of the musical pleasure, as if the sense that a single melody was producing two voices could be magnified when it was achieved by a single hand.

The leap at the opening of Beethoven's *Hammerklavier* Sonata is another example of a musical idea where the physical gesture is an integral part of the significance:

The opening of Beethoven's Hammerklavier *Sonata, op. 106*

Here, too, the effect is difficult to realize accurately with one hand, and almost all pianists are fearful of hitting a wrong note. Many play it with two hands, but this clearly ruins Beethoven's effect. It is a very dangerous and rapid skip, lasting, according to Beethoven's indicated metronome mark, less than one-ninth of a second, with a tremendous sonority given by the spacing and the *fortissimo*. Played as the composer wrote it, it both sounds and looks like a grand and daring leap, and the sense of courage and excitement is communicated aurally and visually. Played with two hands it looks easy, and is easy—and consequently it sounds easy as well.

The feeling that the gesture and the muscular tension within the hand and arm ought to be appropriate to the emotional expression of the phrase is hard to resist. In Mozart's Sonata in D Major, K. 576, for example, the following passage is easier to play if we place the thumb on the F sharp, with the fingering for the first six notes 2 4 1 2 3 5, so that the hand need only stretch a seventh:

From Mozart's Sonata in D Major, K. 576

but I am always tempted to use the more difficult fingering of 2 1 2 3 4 5, where one must span a tenth between the thumb and the fifth finger, because the music stretches a tenth, and the greater length of the line is the basis for its passion and its brilliance. I find it more satisfying to have the experience of playing reflect that emotional tension in the extra physical tension of the hand.

This sense of physically becoming one with the instrument is the origin of the various delusions about the production of a beautiful sonority. Leaving out for the moment the use of the sustaining pedal, there is nothing one can do with a piano except play louder and softer, faster and slower. A single note on the piano cannot be played more or less beautifully, only more or less *forte* or *piano* and longer or shorter. In spite of the beliefs of generations of many thousands of piano teachers, there is no way of pushing down a key more gracefully that will make the slightest difference to the resulting sound. Inside the piano, the elaborate arrangements of joints and springs will only cause the hammer to hit the strings with greater or lesser force. The graceful or dramatic movements of the arms and wrists of the performer are simply a form of choreography that has no practical effect on the mechanism of the instrument, although if it looks more graceful, it may sound more exquisite, not only to the public but to the pianist convinced by his own gestures.

There are indeed different kinds of tonal beauty in piano sound, and each pianist can develop a personal sonority that makes his or her work recognizable, but it does not come from the way any individual note is produced. A "singing" sound on the piano is not given by the instrument but by the way it is exploited with a specific musical phrase, and this exploitation is not mechanical and not a simple matter of technique: it requires at every moment a sense of the music. Beautiful tone production does not exist on the piano apart from the music. A single note on the violin can be beautiful because it can be controlled and made vibrant as it continues to be sustained: a single note on the piano is just a single note. It will appear more agreeable in isolation if it is not too loud and if the pianist does not appear to be thumping it awkwardly. In performing a work on the piano, a beautiful quality of tone is achieved by shaping the melody and molding the harmony and the counterpoint. When that is done right—when the harmonies vibrate and the melody has a unified and convincing contour—the sound is beautiful. In fact, that is how one can produce a beautiful sound even on a piano which may seem at first to give a sonority that is intractably ugly.

The beauty comes essentially from the balance of sound. This balance can be both vertical and horizontal. The vertical dimension is most easily explained in terms of the pure volume of sound of the individual notes within a specific chord. Each chord is more or less rich in sonority according to the way one exploits the vibration of the harmonics or the overtones. The pianist must rely on aural experience: the vibrations in equal temperament are not the same as those in a system of natural tuning. In natural tuning, for example, a minor seventh is an important component of the overtones of a note, and the major seventh a remote harmonic. In equal temperament this is reversed.

The piano is the only keyboard instrument in which one can grandly vary the effects of the harmonics or overtones of a chord at will by balancing the sonority in different ways. I remember that when I was eleven years old and started to study with Moriz Rosenthal, I was astonished when I saw him play a chord several times and realized that he could bring out any individual note of that chord and that his way of doing it was invisible. Composers began to exploit the sonority of the overtones in keyboard music beginning with the invention of the piano. As pianos became larger, this exploitation became more significant. Chopin, Schumann, and Liszt began to use the sustaining pedal not as a special effect (as we find in Haydn and still in Beethoven) but to add a continuous vibration to the sound which helped it carry in the larger spaces, with the gradual development of public concerts. Chopin and Schumann, above all, arranged the accompanying harmonies to make the notes of the melody vibrate. Debussy later created extraordinary effects by this means. A beautiful tone color depends above all on an intuition of the harmonic significance and on an adjustment for the graceful resolution of the more expressive harmonies (even rhythmic nuance enters into a beautiful sonority in this process). What we generally call banging is simply playing the notes of a chord all equally loud with no attempt to adjust for the individual sound of the notes within a chord and the way they resonate.

If it is not, in fact, the relaxed arm and the caressing touch considered essential by so many teachers that produces a good sound, we are obliged to explain why this misconception has been so successful, why, in short, it has actually helped many students over the years to produce a decent tone quality. Balancing the different notes of a chord in a way that brings out the significance of the chord and exploits the harmonics requires the possibility of varying the weight of each finger as one plays the chord. If the arm is stiff and rigid, it becomes almost impossible to achieve this variation: the chord will be played as if by the force of the arm and all the notes will come out more or less the same. Only with a relaxed arm can the muscles of the individual fingers come totally into play, and the sensitivity of the player can make itself manifest. It is this variation and balance of sound that is basically responsible for the tone quality: the relaxed arm does not cause it, but only makes it possible—or, rather, does not prevent the fingers from making it happen. The real source of a beautiful tone quality is the musicianship and intelligence of the performer. This is what should be encouraged in piano pedagogy and not the illusion that there is a purely mechanical or technical method of making a good sound.

There is also another reason, this one purely psychological, that caressing the piano keys with a relaxed touch helps to arrive at a decent tone quality. The physical attitude or the state of the nerves, tendons, and muscles of the body has an inevitable effect on the mood and the interpretation of every passage. The heartbeat quickens and the body tenses during passages of raging fury: the body imitates the music. It goes the other way as well: the music that one produces will inevitably imitate the bodily state. Above all, because of the way so much of the body of the pianist comes into action while playing, this reciprocal mimesis is greater with the piano than with any other keyboard instrument. The gestures of the pianist are inevitably a visual translation of the musical sense.

The vertical beauty of sound depends to some extent on the horizontal dimension, so that one can trace the expressive movement of the different voices within the contrapuntal texture. The glory of the piano is its ability to allow the different voices of the polyphonic structure to interpenetrate each other, shifting the levels from one line to another. The horizontal dimension requires a feeling for the expression latent within the melody and the phrase— and with the bass and inner voices as well. It goes without saying that an accent on a melodic note that sticks out like a sore thumb is immediately felt as ugly. More important is the beauty of sound that comes from recognizing the harmonic meaning within the melody and the curve of its arabesque. In tonal music—at least in the triadic tonality of music from 1600 to 1900—expression is always concentrated in the dissonance. It is the dissonant note within a melody that usually requires at least a slight emphasis, the resolving consonance a softer release except at an emphatic cadence.

The horizontal dimension of sound production exists even when the relation of consonance and dissonance has been weakened, as in dodecaphonic music:

From the minuet in Schoenberg's Suite, op. 25

This opening phrase mimics the relation between dissonance and consonance, between tension and release, and gives the music its neo-classical expression. Piano music from Chopin through Debussy on to Boulez and Elliott Carter depends heavily on the composer's and performer's exploitation of the overtones and the way they act within the phrase. In the first piece of Brahms's op. 119 no. 1, a series of dissonant ninth and eleventh chords are slowly arpeggiated.

The opening of Brahms's Four Piano Pieces, op. 119

Since the harmony consists here of a piling-up of thirds, one of the most resonant intervals, the chord vibrates more and more as the arpeggiation proceeds. Brahms wanted this piece played very slowly, "every note *ritardando,*" to draw out, as he wrote to

Clara Schumann, its full melancholy. The notes of the piano do not vibrate with each other instantaneously but take a moment for the resonance to come into play: the beauty of sound and the full expression in this piece depend on the way this vibration is set in motion.

Much of the tonal beauty of the piano today must be ascribed to the pedal which allows the sympathetic vibrations of the whole instrument to act. Beginning with the 1830s, the almost continuous use of the pedal became the rule in piano playing (although Liszt and his school were more sparing, with a somewhat drier sound). This has had a disastrous effect on the interpretation of Haydn and Beethoven, for whom the pedal was a special effect. Beethoven, in particular, exploited the contrast of a heavily pedaled sonority alternating with dry unpedaled passages.

I have described as mere choreography the gestures that pianists employ in playing, but the choreography has a double practical function. It tells the audience what the performer is feeling when the actual sound may be inadequate for that purpose. I do not wish to defend the more extravagant gestures, but I have found that even the most emphatic final cadence will sometimes not convince an audience that the music is finished; without some kind of visual indication, the applause all performers hope for will be late in coming and more tentative than one would like. The choreography has a purpose for the performer as well. Like singing or grunting when performing, it becomes a way of conducting the music or a kind of self-encouragement. Claudio Arrau's habit, for example, of simulating a vibrato on the more expressive long notes had no effect on the mechanism inside the instrument, but it was a psychological aid to interpretation that perhaps even convinced members of the audience that the note had extra resonance. Graceful gestures can keep the performance relaxed, the way jumping up and down while awaiting a serve loosens a tennis player's muscles. In the case of the pianist, too, the gestures, as I have said, become part of the interpretation.

LISTENING TO THE SOUND OF THE PIANO

PIANISTS—and keyboard players in general—are perhaps the only musicians who do not have to listen to what they are doing.* They often know from a sense of touch alone that they have hit a wrong note. In fact, in my experience one knows that a note will be wrong a split second before striking it, too late to change the movement of the hand or arm. String, wind, and brass players have to hear what they are doing in order to know if they are really in tune, but the pitch of the notes is supplied in advance for pianists by the piano tuner. That is why they can practice on dumb

---

* Drummers in a rock band can often flail away at their instruments with an exhilaration born of pure muscular enthusiasm, but the tympanist in a classical orchestra has to listen carefully in order to muffle the instrument properly after hitting it.

keyboards, invented, I suppose, so as to spare the neighbors. Rachmaninov is said to have learned his own Third Piano Concerto on such an instrument while crossing the Atlantic on a steamer. In the rare cases where the sense of touch does not tell one if the note is right, a glance at the hands will do. But in general pianists neither have to look at nor listen to themselves.

This might seem to be an advantage: it is actually a handicap. Perhaps no musicians—except conductors—are so little aware as pianists of what their performances actually sound like. This is because so much of the sentiment that rightly belongs to the sound of the music is embodied, for pianists and for conductors, in the physical effort, in gesture. I have known conductors who were sensitively aware of what was happening at rehearsals to so lose themselves in their dramatic choreography during the public performance that they did not realize that the orchestra had forgotten everything novel asked for at rehearsal and had gone back to the more familiar phrasing and dynamics of their previous director. Like every other musician, a pianist feels the music with the whole body, but unlike, say, violinists and flutists, more of the pianist's muscles come actively and necessarily into play from the toes to the neck—and with grimaces and hair-tossing may go even higher. Sometimes the emotion, physically realized and experienced, paradoxically does not get translated into sound. ("You could see from his movements and from the expression on his face that he understood the piece and felt deeply about it, but it didn't come out in the playing," one conductor said to me about a pianist with whom he had performed.) Oddly enough, however, the musical sentiment can sometimes, in the end, be transmitted to the public visually solely through the pianist's gestures and attitudes even when it is almost totally absent from the realization in sound. Many members of the audience, in fact, derive their comprehension of the music largely by watching the players or the conductor, and both conductor and pianist can abandon themselves physically to the music without being forced to listen carefully to what is happening.

In a complex passage, rhythm and voice-leading are clear enough to keyboard performers, as we can feel the different lines of the music through our fingertips and along the nerves that run through the shoulders and down the back: slight rhythmic irregularities and unpleasant thickness of sound may reach the ear but never rise to the conscious mind without an effort that not all pianists feel that they have an obligation to make. Part of the pleasure of playing the piano, as we have seen, is purely muscular and almost independent of the sound: the art of the dance will tell us that music may be conceived not only as sound but as movement and physical tension. Gymnastic effort is as essential a part of the music of Bach, Beethoven, and Chopin as it is of Liszt and Balakirev. Often in a Chopin étude, indeed, the intense chromatic harmony will seem to the performer like a metaphor of the fundamental technical difficulty on which the piece is based, as if—quite properly in an étude—the technical difficulty were an end in itself, and the music nothing but a dramatic and emotional expression of the physical effort.

Although string and wind players are used to listening to themselves from the moment they take up their instruments, and the effort to listen becomes unconscious and second nature, pianists forget to do so and have to be reminded. The defect is a curious one, but so serious that in the middle of the twentieth century, as tape machines became easily available and inexpensive, many pianists developed the habit of recording themselves on tape, in order to hear what they were doing. That practice seems to me a disastrous one. It encourages a growing reliance on a mechanical device, when, on the contrary, we need to increase our awareness of what is taking place at the moment of performance. In fact, the problem is a very old one in aesthetics. The best known and most cogent exposition is Diderot's famous *Paradoxe sur le comédien:* it is not the actor who weeps at his own emotion that is the true master, but the one who is objectively aware of his art, stands back, and makes the spectators weep. This is a hard lesson for a pianist, for whom one of the greatest pleasures—one of the reasons for being a pianist, in fact—is forgetting the conscious self in the music. Nevertheless, things are more complex: one must have had the actual subjective experience of losing oneself in the work before one can attain the objective state that enables one to recreate that experience effectively for others in performance.

That objective state can generally be reached only when memory has become almost completely involuntary. When your fingers play the music for you without any need for technical interference from the conscious mind, then you can sit back and listen to yourself and guide the interpretation, trying new effects of tone color, more subtle forms of *rubato*. Perhaps there are performers who can read a piece for the first time with a full perception of everything in the sound, but I have not met any. In playing a piece this involuntary state must be achieved almost throughout: even an adagio goes by too fast to have to ask oneself what the next note will be. Musicians are like those horses that used to draw the milk wagons, who ended up able to go the rounds without the direction of the milkman's reins. (I should say that the memory I am speaking of is not necessarily that of playing without the score. Using the music after one has already studied a work is not like sight-reading the music again; the printed page serves basically to give a series of kick starts to unconsciously stored knowledge.)

I was once made strikingly aware of the confidence derived from this purely mechanical memory. In 1950, with the invention of long-playing records and the use of vinyl instead of the more fragile shellac, small record companies appeared like mushrooms in the musical landscape. One such company had recorded music of Bohuslav Martinu that filled one side of an

LP, and asked me if I knew anyone who played enough Martinu for the other side. "Me," I promptly said, as I had just played in a welcome concert for the first year of Martinu's teaching at Princeton, and had performed a few piano pieces in addition to a cello sonata and piano quintet. Paying for a pianist alone was cheaper than hiring four more musicians, so I had to learn a few new pieces to fill out the side by myself. This was my first record, and the contrast between taping the new pieces and the ones I had previously performed was astonishing. If, after making a take of one of the short works I had already played in concert, the producer asked me if I wanted to return to the control room and listen, I always refused: I already knew whether the take was acceptable or needed another try. With the pieces I had just learned, however, I was never sure until I had listened to the result. It is clear that one should record only the works that one has played several times in public. Within limits, the familiarity given by repeated performance does not remove spontaneity from the playing: on the contrary, the greater ease and the larger awareness of what one is doing allow for new inspiration and a less mechanical rendition. In fact, a long experience of playing a work makes it possible to experiment, to improvise new interpretations in public.

That is why practicing the piano is so often mindless, purely mechanical—and properly so, at least when practicing a difficult passage. There is a different sort of practice, of course, which requires not only intelligence but the ability to listen to oneself: that is the study in balancing the voices within a chord and in shaping the contour of a melody, determining the tone color and the weight of each note. One of the pupils of Artur Schnabel told me that he never heard his teacher practice a difficult passage slowly, but he was struck by the way Schnabel would play one chord of a slow movement over and over, measuring and remeasuring the different components of the harmony. (This might account both for the irrational rhythmic irregularities in his performance of the outer movements of the *Hammerklavier* Sonata and for the exquisite and moving balance of the Adagio.)*

In difficult technical passages, on the other hand, the problem is to disengage the mind and allow the body to take over on its own. This is certainly why Liszt advised his students to read a book while practicing, as Moriz Rosenthal reported. Only when one can play in tempo the skips in *La Campanella* or the octaves at the opening of the development section of the Tchaikovsky Concerto in B-flat Minor while thinking about what to order for dinner, can one pay attention to the interpretation. The situation is not essentially different even with

---

* This is not an attempt to generalize with any authority about Schnabel's technique or about his approach to practicing, which may have varied at any given time as well as throughout his life. His rendition of very rapid soft passages was often extraordinary. I have been told that Horowitz affirmed that the finest performance of the finale of Chopin's Sonata in B-flat Minor (*presto* and *pianissimo* throughout, except for the last bar) was Schnabel's.

works like the Chopin Etudes, for which the tone color is an essential part of the technical difficulty: a provisional decision must be made about the interpretation, and the hands learn to play the passage without any further interference from the taste or intelligence of the pianist. Then, at last, the interpretation can be refined.

The advantage of reading a book while practicing for pure technique alone is that it enables us to forget the boredom of playing a passage over and over again, a dozen, or fifty or a hundred times until the body has absorbed it. Not all books, however, lend themselves equally well to this employment. Poetry interferes subtly with the rhythm of the music, and so does really admirable prose. The most useful, I have found for myself, are detective stories, sociology, and literary criticism. However, any reading matter that distracts the mind without engaging the senses or the emotions too powerfully will work.

A proof of how purely physical the process of learning music can be is the fact that if one practices a passage steadily for a quarter of an hour, an immediate improvement does not always appear. The next day, however, it has suddenly and magically improved as if the labor was validated only by a night's sleep. It is simply that technique works at its best when the involuntary part of the mind takes over more completely. Then consciousness, no longer burdened with the difficulty of hitting the right notes, can assess all the other aspects of performance.

Learning to play the piano is like retracing chronologically the developing history of music. A distinguished Austrian art historian of the turn of the nineteenth and twentieth centuries, Alois Riegl, developed a famous theory that art moves through time in history from the haptic to the optic—that is, from the tactile to the visual. The arts of painting and sculpture started, in primitive ages, with representations where one can trace the lines with one's finger; the introduction of foreshortening in antiquity gave a sense of visual depth; later, the Renaissance invention of perspective unified the whole of pictorial space, and sculpture merged with its architectural setting, no longer simply a frame but part of the representation; Venetian and Baroque coloristic technique later dissolved the individual lines so that the representation was not felt simply as something touched by the hand but as if experienced from a distance; at last, even the objects represented dissolved into visual effects from Impressionism to Cubism (and finally to Abstract Expressionism, which Riegl never saw). This is a grossly simplified account of his thought,* but, in any case, to make the theory work for the history of the visual arts it needed from Riegl himself a considerable amount of adjustment.

It oddly works somewhat more easily for music, where history moves clearly from the tactile to the aural. The mono-

---

* At the end of his life, Riegl felt that the development from the tactile to the visual could be better explained as a movement from the objective to the subjective: the original pair, however, has the slight advantage of taking into account the nature of the perception of the art.

phonic examples of Byzantine and Gregorian chant (and even the monophonic and heterophonic forms of classical Greek music—insofar as we know anything about it) seem to be traceable by the finger like lines through time, and with the introduction of polyphony in the thirteenth century, the music is still felt as separate horizontal lines. The figured bass of Baroque counterpoint, however, intersects the horizontal lines of the voices with vertical components of harmony marching through time. Both the horizontal and vertical elements are fused by Haydn and Mozart into a greater unity, and then begin to dissolve with Schumann and Liszt, where voices merge mysteriously and ambiguously with each other. The dissolution continues with Wagner, in whose music the increasing chromaticism gradually obscures harmonic definition, and is carried almost to the limit by Richard Strauss; Debussy then attacks a too clearly defined sense of rhythmic measuring out by a yardstick; the vertical harmonic markers are removed by Schoenberg and the so-called second Viennese School of his pupils (but the neoclassical Stravinsky undermines the integrity of the harmonic language); finally, many of the basic elements of form—motif, sequential repetition, a steady uniform beat—that seem to have tactile identification (as if one could put a finger on them in a map) are eliminated by Boulez and Stockhausen. This is not merely a development from the simple to the more complex—a sixteenth-century composition by Thomas Tallis or a fugue by Bach may be as intricate as anything by Wagner or Stockhausen. It is a path that leads from the perception of the elements of music taken individually to a sense of the single elements blending together as if they must be understood from the perspective of a greater distance.

Whatever the merits of this historiographic road map, it does follow the way one generally learns to play the piano— with the young learner's experience recapitulating many of the earlier stages of evolution. We start by learning to play simple individual lines in each hand, and eventually combine the two hands and then become acquainted with the phenomenon of the accompanied melody. The harmonic changes of the accompaniment introduce the idea of vertical harmony. We begin to understand how to shape the dynamics of both melody and harmony, which introduces the idea of tone color, and the contrast of textures concentrates our attention on larger aspects of the musical works. We discover how to inflect cut-and-dried aspects of rhythm with the use of *rubato*. Then we find out how to use the pedal: with this, our sense of performance moves radically from the purely tactile to the aural, particularly when we find out that the pedal need not be pushed down to coincide with the notes, but can be syncopated, and can also be varied with the pedal held down only part of the way to damp a fraction of the sound.

I do not wish to make much of a brief for the parallel between the history of music and learning to play the piano, although I believe it is probably true in the large. I have laid it out only to show something more relevant to our general subject: the piano is, until now, the only instrument that allows the performer the direct experience of almost all the important developments and changes in the history of music, from the single line to polyphony, tonal harmony, coloristic dynamics, and the blending together of individual lines; even the twentieth-century interest in exotic or percussive sound effects has been incorporated into the piano repertory, with the use of piano harmonics from Schumann to Elliott Carter, the clusters of Henry Cowell, and the prepared pianos of John Cage. Our experience of learning to play the piano puts us into immediate contact with most of the aspects of western music as they appeared throughout history.

Almost anything can be played on the piano, from troubadour songs to the orchestral works of Debussy, even if a great deal of it does not sound well. The harpsichord *Leçons* of François Couperin are not really effective on the piano, but if no harpsichord is available, the piano is a good way to become acquainted with them. The same thing is true of the masses of Josquin des Prés, the operas of Rossini, the quartets of Haydn, and the symphonies of Mahler. The musicologist Oliver Strunk told me many years ago that he sold his harpsichord in exchange for a piano: "It was too hard to read the tone poems of Strauss at the harpsichord," he explained. Records and tapes have gradually replaced the piano for demonstration in teaching the history of music, but for illustrating details, the piano is still invaluable. Above all, the best way to learn about a work of music is to play it.

The limitations of the piano in reproducing music written for voices or other instruments are triple: the relatively uniform tone color across its range, the difficulty of controlling a sound once it has been struck, and the impossibility of altering a pitch once it has been tuned. The uniformity of tone color is partly a fiction: the tone color of the extreme bass and the extreme treble of the piano are very different. The uniformity is accepted theoretically: with rare exceptions, composers write for the piano as if bass and treble were similar, and performers have to work hard to adjust the sonority and make it balance. On occasion, a composer will exploit the difference between high and low. The beginning of Mozart's Rondo in F Major, K. 494, uses only the high range, and this makes an eloquent contrast even visually on the page with the final bars:

The opening of Mozart's Rondo in F Major (A); and the closing (B)

In the cadenza-like passage added for publication, however, Mozart treats bass and treble as equivalent, and balances them only by adding extra voices in the weaker treble as the stretto continues; it is the pianist who must strive to give the entries of the new voices parallel weight with the opening bass motif:

From Mozart's Rondo in F Major

In the same way, the fourth variation of the Adagio finale of the Sonata in C Minor, op. 111, by Beethoven, juxtaposes bass and treble in a steady *pianissimo* that only enhances the opposition:

*The fourth variation of Beethoven's Sonata in
C Minor, op. 111, bars 1–2 (A) and 9–10 (B)*

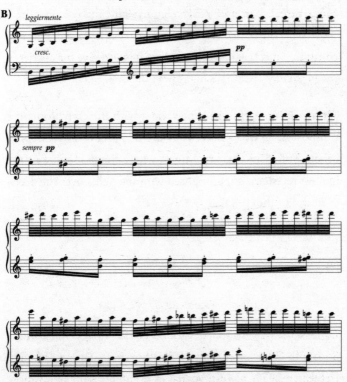

In the third variation, on the contrary, Beethoven pretends that bass and treble are similar, and the performer must effect the necessary balance of weight:

The opening of the third variation of
Beethoven's Sonata in C Minor, op. 111

Sensitivity to register became greater with the early Romantic composers, as we can see from the trio sections of Chopin's Scherzo no. 3 in C-sharp Minor, where the arabesque in the highest register is superimposed with the pedal over the deeper sound of the chorale:

The second theme from Chopin's Scherzo no. 3 in C-sharp Minor

But even Chopin could ignore the different tone color of high and low, above all when he was interested in demonstrating his mastery of traditional polyphonic texture, as in the development of the Sonata in B Minor, op. 58:

*Measures 12–15 from the development of
Chopin's Sonata in B Minor, op. 58*

Not until Debussy do we find a composer always sensitive to the register, and able to exploit it with every note.

What made it possible for composers to refuse to acknowledge the difference on the piano between treble and bass and leave whatever problems arose to be solved by the performer was the fact that the change in tone color over the span of the keyboard is not like the leap from a bassoon to a flute but continuous and very gradual when the instrument is properly voiced. These imperceptible gradations are the result of a deliberate policy of a unified sonority on the part of musicians and instrument makers. All attempts over the history of piano construction to incorporate anything analogous to the picturesque changes of registration in the organ and the harpsichord had little success, were not exploited by composers, and were finally abandoned. Radical contrasts of tone color were traded for the possibility of making a gradual crescendo or diminuendo. This was a decision that took place at the same time as the preeminence accorded to the string quartet over all other forms of chamber music; that, too, emphasized the importance of a unified tone color. Chamber music with wind instruments, while the occasion for several masterpieces, became the exception, an exotic form. That is why the use of colorful sonorities in the orchestra has so often been considered somewhat vulgar, as if calling attention to the sound were paradoxically to detract from the music. The prestige given to pure string sonority is part of the asceticism of nineteenth-century high culture. Contrasts of tone color were given a significantly lower place in the hierarchy of musical elements. This is one reason that only the piano repertory rivals the string quartet as the most respectable medium for private and semiprivate music-making from Haydn to Brahms.

The second limitation of the piano's capacity to realize music written for other instruments is the impossibility of making a crescendo on a sustained note. One can, of course, translate for the piano an orchestral crescendo on a sustained chord by repeating the chord with increasing strength or by playing a tremolo on it, devices occasionally used by Liszt in his transcriptions of orchestral works, but this alters the texture so drastically that it can only be considered a measure of desperation. Diminishing the sound of an already struck note, however, can be partially affected by the use of the pedal. Striking a note staccato while holding the pedal down and lifting the pedal up slowly will create a slow diminuendo, but it works differently for each piano as the contact of the dampers with the strings can be uneven, and it must be rehearsed separately on each new instrument if one wants to make use of the effect. I have always thought that this is what Schumann was thinking of when he wrote a strange pedal indication in *Pierrot* in *Carnaval*. One must play a chord *fortissimo* and detached but with the pedal down, and then play another chord softly; the second chord has four notes in common with the first and two new notes:

The last four bars of Schumann's Pierrot, *from* Carnaval

I presume that the pianist should raise the pedal after the second chord has been softly played. This has the wonderful effect of making a rapid diminuendo of the first chord and, if done right, giving the illusion of a crescendo with the second. Schumann was one of the greatest masters of what one might call *trompe l'oreille.* Nevertheless, the possibilities of diminuendo on a sustained note are limited, and a crescendo strictly impossible (in spite of Schumann's sleight of hand).

One of the great glories of the piano has been its ability to imitate other instruments. In fact, historically, this has been an advantage of the keyboard in general. The organ, of course, has most of its stops based on different instrumental sonorities. The harpsichord as well had the capacity to seem other than it was. Imitations of guitars, trumpets, and drums abound in Scarlatti:

From Scarlatti's Sonata no. 99 (imitating a guitar, A)
and no. 139 (trumpets and drums, B)

(B)

Mozart imitated the triangles and drums of Turkish music in his Sonata in A Major, K. 331:

From Mozart's Sonata in A Major, K. 331

Haydn amazingly discovered how to make the piano sound *pizzicato* at the opening of his Piano Trio in E Major, H. XV: 28:

The opening of Haydn's Piano Trio in E Major

In his Sonata in F-sharp Minor, Schumann directs the pianist to ape the sound of wind instruments in a passage both dramatic and partly facetious that mocks operatic style:

From the Scherzo of Schumann's Sonata in F-sharp Minor

Imitations of the horn, of course, abound in piano music, the most famous being the opening of Beethoven's "Les Adieux." Even more interesting are two bars from the last movement of the Sonata in A Major, op. 101:

From the last movement of Beethoven's Sonata in A Major, op. 101

Here Beethoven directs the pianist to hold down the pedal and play softly so that the horn sounds poetically as if it is coming from a distance.

The pedal makes it possible to inflect the sonority, and compensates somewhat for the rigidity of pitch. The inability to alter the piano's pitch except by tuning has profoundly affected the course of music. The adoption of equal temperament for the piano as the most rational and efficient way of employing all the tonalities forced the adoption of the principle of equal temperament in most of the other instrumental media because of the piano's prestige from the late eighteenth century until the present. It has, therefore, created the tonal system as we know it today, a system based on the perfect triad* and the opportunity of moving to any other perfect triad within musical space. Many musicians have felt this as a species of terrorism, but the introduction of microtones and alternative systems of tuning have had only a very limited success. Perhaps something more may come of them now that the concert grand piano is beginning to seem like a lumbering and embarrassingly inconvenient prehistoric beast on the point of extinction. However, if the piano can deal with so much music that does not properly belong under its control, that is because we look at so much of the music of the past as if it had been conceived with the black and white keys of the piano in the mind of creators of the past ages.

Playing music written for voices or other instruments on the piano may be compared to looking at black and white reproductions—engravings or photographs—of paintings. Before color photography this used to be the way one learned something about pictures in museums too far away to visit. Both piano transcriptions and black and white photography gave information about works in the two arts that was considered satisfactory as long as design and form in painting and pitch and rhythm in music were the fundamental aspects of the two arts. When color in painting and tone color in music usurped some of the authority of design and pitch and became

---

*Like CEG, which defines the central harmony of C major.

basic elements of construction, the two forms of reproduction became more and more unsatisfactory. We can see how this came about in music from the history of transcriptions. When Mozart transcribed his wind sextet in C Minor K. 388 for string quintet (K. 515b), he hardly bothered to change a note, and he felt no need to make the piece more string-like or to make the strings try to imitate a wind sonority—reproducing pitch and rhythm were enough for him. This was the practice that Liszt followed when he transcribed the organ fugues of Bach for the piano: doubling the bass line on occasion was all the alteration he felt necessary (except for transposing a few pitches up or down an octave to make practicable for two hands what had been conceived for one or two manuals and a pedal keyboard). When transcribing the Beethoven symphonies or Berlioz's *Symphonie Fantastique,* however, he was extraordinarily ingenious in his search either to make them sound pianistic or else to make the piano become convincingly orchestral. Liszt once said that the unique example from an important classical work for which he could not find a pianistic equivalent was the opening of the Symphony in G Minor by Mozart.

It is only with the music of the second half of the twentieth century that piano transcriptions began to seem totally inadequate. Timbre was now as important as pitch and sometimes, indeed, more important: the black and white reproduction of the piano transcription no longer did justice to orchestral colors. The piano is no longer an acceptable medium of reproduction of, for example, Edgar Varèse's famous experiments with pure percussion. A ballet on Elliott Carter's great Double Concerto for Harpsichord, Piano and Two Small Chamber Orchestras for the New York City Ballet had to be canceled for that reason. Impressed by Stravinsky, who said of the work, "At last we can speak of an American masterpiece," George Balanchine commissioned the brilliant choreographer Antony Tudor to create a ballet on it, and the first performance was actually announced in the publicity for the following season. But no one could guarantee that other soloists would repeat the recording that Ralph Kirkpatrick and I had made of it, with Gustave Meyer conducting, and it was impossible to make an arrangement for one or two pianos for rehearsal of a piece with two soloists, twelve accompanying musicians in two orchestras and four percussion players with forty-four instruments. Since it was not economically feasible to pay eighteen musicians for every one of the dancers' rehearsals, the project was abandoned. Music had at last developed beyond the possibility of using a piano for rehearsing an orchestral work, and the lack of striking contrast of tone color that had been the piano's greatest advantage had now become a liability. Until this point, nevertheless, the piano could cope however awkwardly with reproducing almost any instrumental group, any form, any style, and any period of music. It was the supreme instrument for gaining musical experience.

The capacity of the piano to absorb or incorporate so much of history creates a genuine problem for the pianist's technique. The accepted repertory goes, with whatever reservations about authenticity, from Bach to Stockhausen. On the most purely technical level—the question of simply pushing the keys down in the right rhythm—no single way of playing the piano can cope with such a wide variety of styles. Even if you have developed a very personal technique, you will not place your hand on the keyboard in exactly the same way when performing Bach and Bartók: different muscles come into play. Your *legato* touch will not be the same in Beethoven and Debussy—or if it is, there is something defective about your sense of style.

I remember how disconcerted I was, after spending some weeks of concentration on Debussy, in order to prepare and record the *Images* and the *Estampes,* to discover an initial and almost willful disinclination of my fingers to play an all-Beethoven program that followed close on the recording sessions. Rendering Debussy's extraordinary art of dissimulating the articulations of the piano sonority, concealing some of the initial percussive impact of the struck notes, developed physical habits of performance that made Beethoven seem odd and ineffective. The world of Debussy is a seductive oasis, and it is hard to leave it after spending many days immersed in its atmosphere. Playing Debussy—or any other composer with a strong and idiosyncratic personality—affects not only one's cast of mind but the physical disposition as well, the way the muscles work and the fingers come into contact with the ivories.

There are two easy escapist answers to the exorbitant demands made on the pianist confronted by the variety of styles. One is to play everything in the same manner, to turn Bach, Chopin, Brahms, and everyone else into Ravel or Prokofiev or into whatever manner or limited number of manners on which you have modeled your technique. It is a great temptation for a pianist with an individual and recognizable personality to filter all music through it, giving everything played a kind of patented character, or, rather, an identifying and marketable stamp. This is not always to the detriment of the music. Hearing Chopin played as if it were Scriabin, as Horowitz often played it, may reveal unsuspected facets.

The second answer is to specialize in one composer, devoting your life and, above all, your reputation to your choice. This choice delights concert agents and record companies, as it makes it possible to sell the pianist as the world's greatest player of Bach or the recognized authority on Mozart or Ravel. Publicity becomes less of a problem. But this form of authority can settle comfortably into a dictatorship. About forty years ago, you could still shock at least the more pretentious members of your audience by presenting Beethoven in a way that differed markedly from the familiar recordings of Artur Schnabel. This specialization, although pleasing to the recording industry, can become tiresome and constraining to any pianist with larger musical interests. Many years ago I heard a performance, admittedly rather odd, of Rachmaninov's Third Piano Concerto by Walter Gieseking, who was generally associated in the public mind with Mozart or Debussy: when asked in an interview why he had chosen to play that work, he replied that he was tired of being expected always to play *pianissimo*.

It is a sad fact that our interpretations of music are conditioned and determined as much by the physical habits of playing we have developed over the years as by any emotional or intellectual understanding of the individual works. But perhaps, on second thought, we should not deplore the pianist's dependence on the body, but celebrate it: music is not limited to sentiment or to the intellect, to emotional commitment or to the critical sense, but engages, at the moment of performance, the whole being. After all, that is why one becomes a pianist.

CHAPTER THREE

THE INSTRUMENT AND ITS DISCONTENTS

PIANOS IMPROVE WITH AGE. The large piece of wood that is the sounding board becomes seasoned with time, and vibrates with greater warmth. It is said that violins improve over the centuries simply through having been played, the wood slowly responding to the many performances. I do not know if this is true, but, after all, an organic substance like wood may undergo gradual change, affected by continuous use. Perhaps that is what happens to pianos, but perhaps it is only that the sounding board gains more resonance with age as long as it does not crack— and it is not accurate, as it is sometimes thought, that a small crack in the sounding board will inevitably cause a deterioration in the quality of sound. Many pianists and technicians claim that the old pianos were better made, and the modern methods of trying to hasten the aging of the wood for the sounding board are not in the long run as beneficial to the tone quality as the old way of simply exposing it for years to the action of Nature. No doubt one day some of the newer less satisfactory instruments will mellow with time, and give the same glowing sound as the older pianos that are so much revered.

Pianos, however, also deteriorate with age. The alterations that result from time and use are more marked and much more disastrous than those suffered by most other instruments. Parts of the action have to be constantly replaced. Not only the strings break, but also the hammers. The metal pins no longer hold the strings tightly enough to remain in tune. The felt on the hammers wears down. The springs of the action lose their tension, the little pieces of cloth and leather that regulate the repetition of the keys wear out, the joints become loose. In too dry an atmosphere, the piano begins to crack and crumble. With an old instrument, we can never be sure that we know what the original sonority was like. In its complexity, the piano is one of the most fragile of instruments. The increased tonal beauty of age is always threatened by imminent decay.

As the piano grew larger throughout the nineteenth century in response to ever more spacious concert halls, it became more ungainly not only to transport but also to regulate. Nothing shows this better than what is called the soft pedal or the *una corda*—the "one string." *Una corda* is now clearly a misnomer. During Beethoven's lifetime, this pedal could shift the entire keyboard to the right so that each hammer would strike only one of the three strings that provide the notes of all the keys above the bass (in the lower regions the strings are so long and thick that only one or two strings are necessary). Beethoven could direct the pianist to play a soft passage in the finale of the Sonata in A-flat Major, op. 110 at first with only one string, and then, by raising the soft pedal slightly, to make a crescendo with two strings, and end up releasing the pedal with the full sonority of three strings. The bigger hammers of the modern instrument, however, require a larger spread in placing the strings so that today there is only a minimal separation of the strings of two notes. Moving the keyboard far enough to the right in order to avoid the two strings on the left would now cause the hammer to strike one string of the next note above, producing a dissonant minor second. Regulating the soft pedal today allows the technician only a few millimeters leeway between one note and the minor second above it, so we can no longer adjust the pedal to strike only one string. Two strings are the minimum: there is therefore no *una corda* any longer but only *due corde*.

With hammers and strings so close together, even the effect of *due corde* is not easy to achieve with perfect uniformity. With continued playing, the hammers do not remain perfectly fixed, and one or more may move a fraction of a centimeter. Unless the distance between the hammers is perfectly coordinated, a few of the hammers will still graze the first string on the left that is supposed to be silent when the soft pedal is used. This means that in a soft passage some of the notes will have a different sound from the others, slightly louder and often more metallic. In my experience, technicians who regulate the sonority or tone of an instrument rarely check the action of the soft pedal. When they do, there are three ways to take care of the problem. The correct way is to align the errant hammer properly so that it is centered like the other hammers exactly under the three strings. However, changing the position of the hammer may result in its having a slightly different sound when it is striking all three strings, so that now the technician would have to readjust the sound of the hammer in its normal position. Months of playing wears grooves into the soft felt of the hammer; if its position is changed, the hammer will strike between the grooves, and this may produce a strange buzz or metallic tingle. A quicker method of regulation is to try and soften the felt on the left side of the hammer, so that its grazing of the string on the left will be less noticeable. Another method—the most makeshift of all—is to adjust the movement of the pedal so that it only moves very slightly to the right, and the third string is grazed by all the keys making a uniform sonority, but considerably diminishing the effectiveness of the soft pedal.

Adjusting the sound of the hammer consists largely of making the thick felt that covers its striking point harder or softer. The hammer hardens with use and the sound becomes more brilliant. When it is unpleasantly harsh, needles are jabbed into the felt to fluff it up and make it less firmly packed. To harden the hammer, on the other hand, the felt can be lightly filed, packing it down and making it more solid, or it can be "doped"—that is, some kind of liquid that hardens as it dries can be placed on it. Making an individual hammer too hard by doping it is dangerous as it becomes more difficult to equalize its sound with the surrounding notes. On one occasion, I had to play the last of Schubert's sonatas, and in the first movement there is a recurring trill very low in the bass that must be played very softly. On the instrument I was using, these notes were so loud that the trill came out as a sinister growl. The technician tried needling the felt without much success: "It's like punching holes in concrete," he complained. Incidents like this one lead to the frequent complaint of performers and technicians that the quality of felt has deteriorated.

The adjustment of the *una corda* depends intrinsically on its purpose, on what one wants to use it for. I have discovered to my surprise that there are two schools of thought on the subject. My own opinion, which I naturally believe to be the only sensible one, is that the *una corda* is intended to provide a different and contrasting sonority with the standard sound of the *tre corde*, a slightly muffled and more distant tone quality.

However, there are pianists who think that the soft pedal is there just to help them play more softly, and they want as little contrast as possible; they therefore demand that the movement to the right be minimal and expect the hammers to graze the third string, giving them a slightly softer sound that differs very little in any other respect from that with the full strings. It is clear, nevertheless, from Beethoven's frequent directions for the use of the *una corda*, for example, that he made a great distinction between a *pianissimo* with the soft pedal and one without. With the *una corda* he generally prescribed a sonority that he described as *mezza voce*, or "half voice." A century later, on the last page of *Scarbo* (the third and final piece of *Gaspard de la Nuit*), Ravel demanded that the pianist play *mezzo forte* with the soft pedal held down, and this produces a wonderfully hoarse, muffled and sinister effect that can be achieved only if the soft pedal acts on only two strings. In any case, the development of the piano from 1800 to the present has already resulted in the loss of the contrast between one and three strings, and I think it is a mistake to minimize the action of what is left of the soft pedal and take away still more of the variety of tone quality available to pianists of Beethoven's time.

The tone quality of a piano is determined by the shape of the hammers. If the top of the hammer is too flat, it will block some of the resonance of the string: struck with force, the note may have an initial loud percussive impact, but some of the sustaining power will be lost. Shaping the hammers is a fine art: great technicians are as scarce, or scarcer, than great performers. It also requires a remarkable musical sense to "voice" the piano, to regulate the sound so that all the hammers strike with equal effect. As I have said, the sonority of the piano is supposed to be uniform from treble to bass, but this is something of a myth: the treble is very different in tone quality from the bass. The change over the keyboard must, however, be gradual. Contiguous keys should ideally have the same tone quality, should be similarly voiced.

In reality, this is impossible to achieve with perfection. The wood of the sounding board is an organic substance, and is never absolutely uniform. Some pitches on the piano will resonate with greater or less power and even with a different quality of sound. A good technician may compensate for much of this disunity, but can never iron out all the discrepancies. Nor would it be a good idea to try and remove every irregularity: each instrument has a personality of its own. (In most cases, the only way to achieve more perfect uniformity is to make the piano much less brilliant over its whole range, and this results in a mushier tone quality.) One brilliant technician in Holland, who had rebuilt the action of a Steinway concert grand I was using for three recordings of Schumann's works, remarked to me that he could try for greater uniformity, but that the piano would lose some of its character. He was justifiably proud of his instrument. "Tell me which notes bother you," he said, "and I will fix them." A slightly harsh low F sharp did not make much difference in the Fantasie in C Major, op. 17, but it was a continuous irritant in the Sonata in F-sharp Minor, which I recorded the next day. He could, indeed, fix a single note with almost lightning speed, and not hold up the process of recording.

A pianist should cultivate a certain humility before a really fine technician. It is not always easy to determine irregularities of tone quality with complete precision. In the first place, one must be sure of striking the notes in exactly the same way: instinctively, pianists almost always adjust the force slightly, particularly if they think that a note is too brilliant. In fact, to test for uniformity, one must strike the keys in an insensitive manner that would be thought unmusical. Most troubling of all, however, is that a note will not always have the same quality of sound to someone sitting in front of the keyboard as it will to someone standing up or listening to one side of the instrument; in addition, a microphone may pick up slight but exasperating differences in tone quality that may be impercep-tible to a concert audience. In any case, before I complain to a technician about the sound of a note, I try the sound standing as well as sitting before the keyboard, and have been aston-ished at the difference that can make.

Many aspects of the quality of the sound of a piano can be altered. What cannot be changed is the decay of sound: this comes from the sounding-board, and is, to my mind, what defines the intrinsic beauty of an instrument. The initial impact of a note is always strong and slightly percussive, even with a soft note: on a machine that measures decibels, the needle will jump instantly to the right as the note is struck and fall immediately back toward the center of the dial. It will then, if the note is sustained, move slowly and gradually back to zero. It is the second drop that determines the decay of sound: the longer the note can be sustained before it finally disappears, the greater will be the singing capacity of the instrument. The decay on a concert grand tends to be longer than that on the smaller instruments: for this reason the belief that it is possible to play more softly on a smaller instrument is false. Played so softly that the note just sounds or "speaks," a long decay of sound will sustain this minimal sonority with great effect within a soft *cantabile* melody. With a shorter decay, on the other hand, one must give the note more of a thump to make sure it will carry over and make a sustained melodic line. With the larger instrument, therefore, one can often play more softly: the sound will carry in a very large hall with good acoustics no matter how softly one plays if the piano will sustain a soft sound. The tendency for concert societies to rent a smaller instrument for a smaller hall may have its economic justification, but it makes no sense in terms of the effectiveness of the performance. (It should be remarked here that piano companies today take less care of their smaller models like the Steinway B, six feet in length, and reserve most of their solicitude for the nine-feet-long standard concert grand.) To test for

the decay of sound, I generally try this passage from Chopin's
Polonaise-Fantaisie:

The opening of Chopin's Polonaise-Fantaisie

If the G of bars 4 and 5, in the right hand, without having
been hit with an unreasonable force, is still sounding with a

true melodic sense after one has released the other notes of the chord, then the decay is ideal, and one can realize the effect that Chopin had in mind.

The right-hand and middle pedals on the piano may need adjustment but are rarely as much of a nuisance to regulate as the soft pedal. The sustaining pedal on the right can cause trouble when it is too responsive, and many pianos today are made deliberately with an oversensitive right pedal. Rest your foot even lightly on it when playing one of the latest models and it immediately starts to function. This means that you must keep your foot away from the pedal when not using it or keep it lifted a fraction of an inch above the pedal which creates a strain on the ankle that can distract the performer during playing. On the older pianos the pedal had a certain resistance, and this also made it easier to judge how far one wanted to push the pedal down. Using only what is called a half-pedal that raises the dampers slightly but still allows them a minimum contact with the strings results in a delicate wash of sound that sustains without blurring. One can also make a strange and dramatic effect with the sustaining pedal: if you hold the pedal down and play a very loud chord with many notes, particularly some of them in the bass, and then release the pedal very slowly, as the dampers just begin to graze the strings the piano will often produce a snarling aggressive noise. This is obviously not an effect that would be welcome in Chopin or Mozart, but Pierre Boulez asks for it in one of the movements of his Third Piano Sonata. The action of slowly raising the pedal (or lowering the dampers) is idiosyncratic on each piano, and this effect must be carefully rehearsed in order to achieve the desired snarl.

The pedal in the middle, which does not exist on all brands of piano, largely came into its own in the twentieth century: it sustains only the notes that are actually being held down as one lowers this pedal. That enables one to single out certain notes for a long sustained sound, meanwhile playing the rest of the texture either dryly or with continuously changing pedal to avoid an intolerable blur. The early nineteenth-century instruments did not need this pedal, as each harmony was much weaker, dying away more quickly and, even when the sustaining pedal was used, more easily pushed aside and replaced by the new harmonies as the piece went on. (It is evident that Schumann, for example, could use more pedal with impunity in his compositions than we can today, although his habit of keeping his foot down on the pedal for long stretches seems to have astonished and even exasperated his contemporaries.) Twentieth-century composers have made extensive use of the middle pedal, and, in fact, have found it most useful to achieve an effect derived from an invention of Schumann: that is, to hold down certain notes silently, and then play a passage over or under these notes which makes their harmonics or overtones vibrate, creating a strange, eery and diaphanous sound. (In *Carnaval* Schumann directs the pianist to pedal a very heavy texture in the bass *fortissimo,* hold down the keys of a dominant seventh chord silently—that is, without allowing the hammers to strike the strings—and then raise the pedal: the new dominant seventh harmony rises out of the previous thick texture and makes an ethereal transition to the next piece.) It is largely by the use of this pedal that composers have been able to enlarge the repertory of piano sonorities. Unfortunately, not all tuners know how to adjust the middle pedal, at least not in small towns, and once in South Africa I had to change the program and play Mozart instead of Boulez for this reason: it did not raise a large protest from the members of the audience, but only a gentle reproach later from a few amateurs of modernism.

Perhaps the most delicate part of the mechanism of the piano is the repetition. That was the major problem for the inventors of the piano: how to catch the falling hammer fast enough after a note has been struck to allow it to be repeated at once. Research continued to be done on this problem for much of the twentieth century. Even today, after all the improvements effected over almost two hundred years, if the action is not regulated with great care, a note will often tend to jam after being repeated rapidly five or six times. This can be disastrous for the rapid guitar strumming effects of a piece like Ravel's *Alborado del Gracioso* from *Miroirs,* and the trills in earlier compositions can suffer as well. It has always seemed to me bizarre that an instrument that has grown to such monstrous proportions since the eighteenth century should need such delicate and fussy adjustment, and become not simpler but more difficult and complex to put into good shape.

There is also the curious problem of too much repetition: when the action of the piano is not in the best shape, a note played softly may bounce back and play a second time. This was an effect that Glenn Gould liked, somewhat perversely I thought; in any case, his records have many examples of a soft note sounding rapidly twice, the second time played by the instrument itself with no help from the pianist. In Gould's case, this came about because he reduced the resistance of the key to being struck. There is a specific point of resistance called the aftertouch where the key needs a slight extra push that Gould largely eliminated: this enabled him to achieve extraordinarily even, soft rapid passage-work, but it also caused the hammer at times to strike twice very quickly and gently. The unwanted repetition can also occur if the level of the hammers is too low, and instead of being gently held in check as they fall, they tend to bounce back when the note is played very softly. This defect is not always discovered by the tuner, who will rarely try to play as softly as the pianist. On one occasion, many years ago in Orchestra Hall in Chicago, a tuner who did not know how to deal with the problem said, "Look! When I play a note, it only sounds once. You must be putting your hands down wrong." I remember shouting back indignantly that the principle of playing the piano was that when you pushed the key down once, it played only once. I stormed into the Steinway office the next week in New York and said I had just been in Chicago, but before I could explain further, I was told hastily that they were sending someone to Chicago in a few days to find out what was going on.

Breaking a string on a piano is slightly more of a problem than the general public realizes, as a new replacement string will not stay in tune very long at first. On the eighteenth-century pianos, the broken strings were no doubt the pianist's fault, as the instruments had a limited resistance to the use of force. Beethoven was renowned for smashing not only strings but hammers. On today's sturdier pianos, a broken string is generally due solely to long-term wear. In any case, I have only broken a string once during a performance (in the first movement of Brahms's Concerto no. 2 in B-flat Major), but I did have a string broken for me by the tuner before a New York recital; unfortunately, he broke a high B flat just before I was to play Beethoven's Sonata in B-flat Major op. 106 (it is almost always the weaker high strings that break). The way a modern piano is strung (except for the lowest notes in the bass), the six strings of two contiguous notes are formed by only three strings, each starting at one tuning pin, then looping down around a hitchpin below the bridge and returning to a second tuning pin. The second string of the three will have one side tuned to one note and the other side tuned to the note next to it. The string that broke did double duty for two B-flat strings, so there was only one string left on that note crucial to the piece on the program. Replacing the broken string would have meant that it would have been audibly and jarringly out of tune five minutes after the beginning of the concert, but by forming a loop knot at the end of the unbroken part of the string and placing it on the hitchpin the technician was able to restore one of the two missing B flats. Since it was already properly stretched, it remained fairly well in tune for the concert. A broken string should not be blamed on the pianist: the modern concert grand is built to stand up to a lot of punishment—there is, after all, a lot of pressure exerted on the frame by the strings, ten tons, in fact.

One menace that threatens the peace of mind of a concert pianist is returning to an instrument reserved in advance some time before and finding that another pianist has asked a technician to alter its character, to make it more or less brilliant. To change it back to its previous sound is sometimes a delicate job. It is not hard, as I have said, to make a piano less brilliant, nor does it take very long: stabbing the felt of the hammers with needles will do it very quickly. Restoring the brilliance to an instrument from which it has been removed, however, is a more delicate and lengthier job. It requires tact and patience, and a technician with a sensitive ear and hands. Having experienced this problem—that is, having chosen a piano for a future recording date and discovering some weeks later that another pianist (for whom I have the greatest admiration and who shall therefore remain nameless) selected the same piano for a performance in Carnegie Hall but had had its sound considerably softened—I have developed a prejudice against any attempt to change the character of an instrument. I have often asked for the voicing to be made more even and more balanced, or for a range of half a dozen notes to be made more compatible with the rest of the keyboard, but I have never demanded any wholesale change over the whole piano. This would, I believe, be justifiable only if one was the sole user of the instrument over a considerable length of time.

The most common problem with voicing is that the area of the second octave above middle C tends to be weaker on many pianos. A long time ago, when I first played in London, I complained about the weakness of these notes to the technician. "Ah," he said, "those are the notes that are played the most often [it is indeed true that the principal melodic line is generally placed in that range] and the brilliance eventually comes back with use. We deliberately voice those notes with less brilliance." Increased use may, indeed, be the best way to return brilliance to an action, but it is not much help if you have to play that evening. This was an example of the prudence and moderation for which the English were then famous. It is encouraging to report that the London office of Steinway modified their policy later, and voiced evenly throughout. On one occasion, in fact, when an instrument that I had used many times had been rebuilt with new hammers, it was not sent out for a few months but was kept in the office of the chief technician, Bob Glazebrook, an artisan of superb craft and great generosity: knowing how much I loved the piano, he asked me to practice on it for a number of days in his office, in order to season it naturally before it was used again in a large hall.

At the beginning of the twentieth century, pianos used for public performances frequently were shipped long distances without considerable cost (the charges, indeed, for well-known artists were often borne by the piano company). Pianos were shipped across the American continent and even overseas from Europe to America and back. This meant that many pianists were able to play almost all the time on the instrument with which they were familiar. Costs began to rise by the middle of the century. Artur Rubinstein, for example, by the 1960s no longer used the same instrument in New York and California. It was possible to insist on the instrument one preferred within a range of a few hundred miles of a large city, but for longer distances the cost was now prohibitive. Some lesser piano companies would pay the expenses for the few artists who were willing to settle for their instruments, but Steinway would not. Perhaps the last pianist in the twentieth century to afford the luxury of playing only the same instrument in all performances was Vladimir Horowitz, although for many years Arturo Benedetti Michelangeli insisted on shipping an instrument for his concerts. If he was forced to use another instrument when his was not available, his own technician would make substantial and disconcerting alterations to it.

It should be realized that the technical accuracy one finds in recordings of many pianists from the 1920s is at least partly due to the benefits of being able to play the same piano, and to not having to get used constantly to different actions with different weights, different resistance, and different configurations of sonority. Today, going from a new piano which is somewhat stiff and often voiced for harsh brilliance to an older piano with a much looser response and a more mellow quality is like changing from a Mack truck to a Ferrari. The advantage of always playing the same instrument cannot be overestimated. A piano on which one has played a dozen times is an old friend, even if that piano has other friends as well: back on the 1960s, a whole generation of American pianists recorded on the same instrument, Steinway No. 199. It was used by Gary Graffman, Jacob Lateiner, Leon Fleisher, and myself. There must have been others as well. It was a beautiful instrument with a long decay of sound, and a sonority that combined warmth and brilliance. When the action finally wore out, the piano was sold, although if the company had really had a heart, they would have rebuilt it.

In the last years of the nineteenth century as pianos were getting bigger and louder, the actions became heavier and stiffer, and pianists had to push the keys down to a greater depth. This demanded more muscle power, as if pianism had not already become sufficiently athletic during the youthful years of Franz Liszt. Nothing reveals the greater stiffness of the modern action more than the octave *glissandi* written for the piano by Haydn, Beethoven, Weber, and Brahms: easy to execute on the instruments of the period, they now require a special technique and are abnormally difficult on some instruments when the resistance is more than standard. (An octave *glissando* is played by starting an octave with the thumb and fifth finger and then dragging or sliding the hand along the white keys; for practical reasons, right-hand octave *glissandi* generally go down, left-hand go up.) When my teacher showed me how to do this, he told me to practice it for only ten seconds a day for a week: "more than that," he said, "and you will get a blister on your fifth finger." Played very rapidly, an octave *glissando* is relatively simple. It is only at a moderate tempo that it becomes difficult on today's pianos. The *glissandi* in Beethoven's Piano Concerto no. 1 in C Major and in Brahms's Variations on a Theme of Paganini are properly played at a moderate tempo: in the Beethoven concerto, in fact, if the tempo is not moderate and precise the conductor will find it awkward to bring in the orchestra exactly in the middle of the pianist's scale in octaves (most pianists use two hands here, but then the low G in the bass cannot be timed to come exactly in the middle of the scale with the entrance of the orchestra, which makes it more dramatic). In the Brahms a very fast tempo will result in a smear instead of the exact rhythm indicated by the composer. (The octave *glissandi* demanded by Stravinsky in his arrangement for piano of

Octava glissandi: (A) Brahms's Variations on a Theme of Paganini;
(B) Beethoven's Piano Concerto no. 1 in C Major

Petrouchka, Scene III, are more easily negotiable because they are intended to be played very rapidly.)

A simple single-note *glissando* is more difficult on the black keys than on the white since it is hard to slide on keys that are that far apart: the black-key *glissandi* in Bartók's Sonata for Two Pianos and Percussion were solved neatly by one pianist, Leonid Hambro, who played them with his wallet, left on the piano within easy reach of the keyboard. I do not think that any composer has ever asked for octave *glissandi* on the black keys, but there is a recording by Moriz Rosenthal of Chopin's *Black-Key* Etude in which he plays the short octave passage in both hands *glissando:* it hurts my hands just to think about it.

It is the heavier action of modern pianos that has made all *glissandi* more onerous. Robert Casadesus refused to play the *glissandi* in thirds and fourths in Ravel's *Alborada del Gracioso* after seeing blood on the keys at one performance. The older instruments, lighter in action and, at least in the early nine- teenth century, with slightly narrower keys, were less destruc- tive of the performers' cuticles. There are ways of making octave *glissandi* less fearsome. Before the famous example in the last movement of Beethoven's *Waldstein* Sonata, Rudolf Serkin used to lick his thumb and fifth fingers quickly in order to facilitate the slide. A more efficient, or at least less ostenta- tious method was demonstrated by a piano technician in Minneapolis. I had to play all five Beethoven concertos in three successive evenings with the Minneapolis Symphony. The first program had the first and fourth concertos. On the first piano

I tried (it was already in the hall), I could play the octave *glissando* in the first movement with ease, but the instrument was not one on which a real *cantabile* could be achieved: the sonority was both harsh and a little dead. A second piano was available that had a lovely and gracious sound, but it was almost impossible to play the *glissando* on it in strict time. I said that I wanted to use two pianos for that concert, the first one for Concerto no. 1, and the more beautiful sounding instrument for Concerto no. 4. The technician (whom I had known in New York before he emigrated to Minnesota) said he would make the *glissando* possible on the finer piano. Lifting out the long piece of wood that stands in front of the ivories, he showed me the metal pins under each key, and added a touch of lubricant on the right side of each one (the *glissando* descends, so the lubrication is necessary only on the right): the passage became at once much more satisfactory. I need not add that one should use only a lubricant that evaporates and does not leave a sticky residue.

After this summary account of what can go wrong with a piano, it should be admitted that a fine performance can be achieved on an instrument that is not what one would hope for. Busoni once said that there are no bad pianos, only bad pianists. That may be true enough, but a defective piano takes away much of the delight of the performer, and for the proper functioning of the world of music, the musicians should derive as much pleasure as the public. What is more troubling for pianists to face is the fact that many of the irregularities that bother us are largely imperceptible to an audience, which does not consciously realize that one note lacks brilliance and another is too harsh. Moreover, a note in which one of the strings is slightly out of tune makes a less agreeable sound, and the audience is more apt to think that the pianist is insensible to tone quality than to understand that one of the unisons is flat.

One final small inconvenience for concert pianists might be mentioned here. A conscientious tuner will often clean the keyboard when the tuning is finished; while this removes the presence of the slightly sticky dried sweat from rehearsal and tuning, it also makes the keys more slippery, eliminating traction. I am told that when this happened Artur Rubinstein used to call hastily for rosin to put on his fingers, as a violinist applies it to the bow before playing, or else he sprayed hair spray over the keys.

CHAPTER FOUR

CONSERVATORIES AND CONTESTS

IT IS MUCH HARDER TO FORGET music than to remember it. Paul Valéry, in his guise of Monsieur Teste, claimed that he had a system for recalling everything he wanted to know but had never found a way to forget what he preferred not to remember. This is even more the case with music than with literature or with life in general. Most resistant is the music one has learned when young. There are pieces I used to play when I was fifteen that I never wish to perform again, tunes I have heard and would like to forget, but I have not been able to wipe them from my memory. My head is filled with the unneeded clutter and debris of earlier years.

Later in life music becomes both more difficult to memorize and easier to forget. Small children with a gift for music commonly have an amazing memory. There are many stories of children who when starting piano lessons were thought to be able to read music, but had not in fact acquired the skill: they had heard the teacher play a piece once and could repeat it without mistake. Piano teachers have had to learn not to play a new piece for the more talented beginners. I know a cellist who at the age of ten started playing the clarinet in the school band, without being able to read music. "I just played what the next boy played," he said. "After a year, I decided it was foolish not to be able to read music. It took me fifteen minutes." (Learning to read music, often considered by editors and publishers as an esoteric skill, is indeed a simple matter. I suspect, however, that an astonishing percentage of today's audience for classical music is, in fact, musically illiterate. That, of course, does not prevent appreciation: probably a good proportion of Sophocles' audience in ancient Athens was analphabetical; do we know how many of the groundlings in the public at Shakespeare's Globe Theater could read?)

I must insist on the extraordinary tenacity of works committed to memory in childhood and adolescence. After one reaches voting age, not only does memory register a text more slowly but also blurs it more rapidly. When I was sixteen, I could sight-read a Chopin Nocturne once and then play it by heart. I hasten to add that this experience is not unusual for young pianists. What is more significant, I can quickly recall almost every work that I learned before I was twenty, and I believe many other pianists have also found this to be true. It has been a long time since I needed to look at the score of, say, Beethoven's Fourth Piano Concerto or the *Appassionata* except to make sure that I had paid as close attention to Beethoven's phrasing as I have come to do since the days when I first approached these works. It now requires a special effort for me to change a fingering that I adopted when I first learned a piece as a child. Rethinking the phrasing, dynamics, and tempo is easier than revising the fingering: what is purely technical must become mostly unconscious, routine, while at least a partial alertness is beneficial to an interpretation. Yet if I committed a work to memory only five years ago, I must go back to the music today not quite as if I had never seen it, but nevertheless as if it were a relatively unfamiliar piece. There are methods for training memory later in life (Gieseking developed one and so did Dimitri Mitropoulos, who even memorized the name of every member of an orchestra new to him before the first rehearsal), but they do not work for everyone. With advancing age, as is well known, memory becomes doubly uncertain: above all, what begins to fail is confidence in one's memory, the assurance that the next note will follow with no conscious effort. For a while, Richter would bring the score on to the stage, and place it on the floor next to the piano chair; in his last years he surrendered completely and opened the score on the music rack, as Myra Hess had done at the end of her life.

The earliest and most powerful memories are involuntary ones, built in physically, so to speak. For this reason it is a great advantage to learn to play the piano very young, and in fact most professional pianists started when they were four or five. There is a famous story about Nadia Boulanger, the teacher of so many important American composers during the 1920s and 1930s: asked by a friend to recommend a piano teacher for his son, she first wanted to know how old the boy was. "Seven," replied her friend. "Too late," was Mlle. Boulanger's rejoinder. Of course it is never too late to learn to play the piano for one's own pleasure, but playing the piano professionally is like walking a tightrope: start too late in life and you fall off. Not only do professional pianists, like circus performers, begin very early, but they generally know almost from the start that they will make their career as pianists. There are a few exceptions: Richter is said to have decided to pursue a professional career later than early childhood, but in his teens he was already the rehearsal pianist at the Odessa Opera. Harold Bauer chose a professional life as a pianist in late youth. He had intended to be a violinist, but he already played the piano so impressively that Fritz Kreisler advised him to make that his career. (There is in existence somewhere in the world a recording of Kreisler and Bauer playing together, with Bauer at the violin and Kreisler at the keyboard.)

Ideally you should become acquainted as soon as possible with a good part of what will be the repertory for the rest of your life. It is certainly not necessary to master all the works at once. It is astonishing how fast you can learn a work that you have sight-read a few times over the years even if it is several decades since the last reading. The mind and the body retain something of even these casual encounters that can resurface long afterward. Another advantage of cultivating a fleeting contact with many works is that it is impossible to know with any conviction if you can bring something personal to a work unless you have first tried to play it. The tendency today to substitute listening to records for sight-reading results in our comprehension of the music being filtered through someone else's ears: even the composer does not know all the interpretative possibilities of a new work before trying it out.

The keyboard repertory is vast, much of it relatively unexplored territory. No other instrumentalist is offered so wide a range of possibilities as the pianist. By contrast, for example, the complete solo viola repertory worth playing can, I should imagine, be mastered in a few months. The pianist's repertory is largely late eighteenth through early twentieth century, but it was gradually broadened to include the earlier composers Bach, Scarlatti, Rameau, Handel, and some of their contemporaries, and it continued to grow throughout the twentieth with music recently composed, although more and more slowly in the final decades. Merely becoming aware of what is out there is a prodigious task. Unfortunately the two institutions that control the outset of almost every pianist's career, the music school and the piano competition, tend to hinder the development of the direct and experimental approach to the repertory that would be most profitable.

There is no question that the best conservatories and the music departments of universities are aware of the problem and do the best they can: excellent courses in piano repertory are offered in order to make students aware of the extraordinary possibilities; sight-reading is actively encouraged. The difficulty, nevertheless, is inherent in the system. A conservatory or a music department must give a diploma generally after four years of study, a certificate of proficiency, a document that guarantees that the student has been respectably educated. Examinations can be given in courses like solfège, counterpoint, and music history which can seem subsidiary to many piano students and a downright nuisance to some. Most of them wish understandably to concentrate on the piano, and specifically on the solo repertoire. The fact that few of them, even the most ambitious, will eventually have a solo career is irrelevant: an education in the arts, and in the other humanities and sciences as well, ought to offer both a hope for the future and the right to study what interests the individual most deeply.

The only way to test for proficiency in playing the piano is to have the student play a recital. Accordingly the system universally applied is to require each student to play one recital each year, and, if it is not a disaster, then move on to the next year. (Some places only demand a recital in the last year or in each of the last two years.) This cut-and-dried plan of a single recital each year is not always the best policy for every student: some need to develop their technique more slowly, enlarge their acquaintance with the possibilities of the repertory, get rid of poor habits acquired from earlier bad teaching. Some even still need to find a style of playing and a technique that suits their temperament and their hands. The single recital in the final year can often be even more constraining, as if the student must sum up the years of study with an hour and a quarter of playing time. In most institutions, however, the system is inexorable. At the end with diploma in hand, most young pianists are pushed out into the world to make their way as best they can. To show for their four years of study, most of them have a repertory of at best only four programs: this essentially amounts to about five hours of piano music.

Whether the student succeeds in achieving a professional career as a soloist, or ends up teaching, or leaves music and becomes a computer programmer or an investment banker and plays the piano for pleasure only makes little difference as far as the value of the education is concerned: for amateur or professional, the life of a pianist is more rewarding the larger the repertory. The more music one can actually recreate for oneself, even informally, the richer one's experience of the art becomes.

In all fairness I must add here a personal note. My first-hand knowledge of the teaching system is limited. I left the Juilliard School at the age of eleven to study privately, so I was deprived of a conservatory education—or escaped it, depending on how you look at it. The benefits of conservatory training are obvious: the contact with musicians of your own age and the possibility of playing a great deal of chamber music. The disadvantage is equally evident: the lack of freedom to develop at one's own pace and the constraint of the stylistic standards imposed by a teaching staff and by the administration—even when both are exceptionally benevolent, the pressure is always applied, often unwittingly.

Many years ago, however, I had to take over the advanced piano class at the University of Texas at Austin for one spring term. I came with only two or three weeks notice after the sudden death of the professor. I inherited a remarkably talented group of a dozen students, many of whom had already won a prize in a piano competition. All of them had to play a recital or give a performance by April of that term, and the deadline for changing any of the programs had already passed. Essentially I had to help them get through their chosen programs: any attempt to help them make basic improvements to their technique or discover new possibilities of interpretation was limited and, indeed, out of place. (I remember having to stay with one student for four hours showing him how to practice Chopin's Etude in thirds: he ended up able to play it quite well, but it did not, in the end, alleviate some of his basic technical problems.) I did, however, try to find out on arrival what the students' knowledge of the repertory was, and asked how many had read through all the sonatas of Beethoven: four of them had. How many had read the sonatas of Schubert? None.

It would take only about eight hours to read through all the Schubert sonatas—less if you skip the repeats—and about another five to become acquainted with everything else he wrote for the solo piano: the equally great repertory of Schubert for one piano four hands would take only a little longer, but it needs a friend as enthusiastic as oneself. Sight-reading comes more easily to some pianists than to others, but it is an art that is developed almost entirely by practicing it. The only stimulus one needs is curiosity. In about six months of sight-reading for three hours a day, one could go through most of the keyboard music of Bach, Handel, Mozart, Chopin, Schumann, Mendelssohn, and Brahms. Another few months and one can add Haydn, Debussy, and Ravel. Another hour and a quarter would suffice for all of Schoenberg's piano music (or two hours if you have more trouble reading it at first), and an hour and a half will get you through Stravinsky, including the works for piano and orchestra, and ten minutes each for the solo piano works of Anton von Webern and Alban Berg. For a pianist who begins to play at the age of four, not to have done all this by the age of twenty is to create a handicap that will last for the rest of life. Those are the years when the experience of reading an unfamiliar work can most easily set the spirit on fire with new possibilities. Above all, it establishes a basic and permanent fund of knowledge. And in the next years, one can become reasonably well acquainted with the symphonic, chamber, and operatic worlds, through listening, score-reading, or piano reductions. It is not the dogmatic application of knowledge or of rules of style that deepens an interpretation but the years of experience that transmit themselves unconsciously to performance.

By its nature, an institution must favor routine over individual eccentricity. It cannot set a value on the quality of a student's experience or the potential for future expansion of this experience: it can only judge present proficiency. Therefore it is only as a sideline that it can encourage a breadth of direct and intimate knowledge of the repertory and the long history of the performance practice of music. To justify giving every graduate a certificate, the school must demand proof that each candidate can not only perform a standard piece but is able to produce a performance in the accepted manner. The most foolish traditions, however, may become accepted and easily entrenched. On another of the rare teaching assignments in which I found myself, I had to coach a performance at a chamber music festival of Beethoven's *Ghost* Trio for piano and strings, op. 70 no. 1. The slow movement, marked *Largo*, is most often played at a ridiculously slow tempo, as if the *Largo* was intended to be determined not by the opening bars, which move from quarters to eighths to sixteenth notes, but by the later sections where Beethoven reaches the sinister and spectral shimmer of sixty-fourth notes. When I observed that the tempo should be almost twice as fast as the one the students had selected, they protested that if they played it any faster, they would fail the exam for which they were preparing the work. This was about fifteen years ago; since then, it has gradually been accepted that many of the tempos of Beethoven's slow movements were probably intended to be faster than we once believed.

Eventually, I presume, this will result in a new orthodoxy. We must not assume that it will necessarily lead to an improvement. I do not challenge the idea that there is a correct tempo for a work, at least during certain periods of history when musical style was relatively homogeneous. Nor do I challenge the belief that we can sometimes, if not always, determine what that tempo was. What I regret is the failure to realize that it is often effective and advantageous to play a work at the wrong tempo. Many great performers have given wonderful and illuminating renditions of works at tempos that they themselves could believe was the one the composer intended only by cultivating a delusion. A student should decide on a tempo not because it is accepted by the academy, but because it is effective or because it suits his or her individual sensibility. When the conservatory imposes a respectably correct performance with the rigor of authority, it not only encroaches on the indispensable liberty of the students, but hinders their artistic development. Nevertheless, an institution must insist on standards, and to ask any large and well-entrenched institution to apply these standards with suppleness and intelligence is to create a burden unrealistic for a department of piano instruction.

A good deal of pedagogy today is channeled through what is called a master class. A figure of some fame or notoriety is asked to hear a number of students perform before an audience of other students and, sometimes, curious outsiders, and to give a public lesson. There is a certain amount of illusion associated with the practice: like group therapy, it is a way of earning more money per hour and doing less work. The question could be put in this way: whom does one teach during a master class, the performing student or the attendant public? In most cases it has to be the public rather than the performer, the latter playing the role of the sacrificial victim.

The best method of teaching is to practice with a student, or to demonstrate how one practices and then watch the student work until the passage comes right. Before the student's technique is almost completely formed, this is the only way, and requires a lot of patience. But if the performer in a master class has some deficiency (and this need not be only a question of the right notes at the right speed, but could be a difficulty of rhythmic sense or tone quality), making him or her practice in public is humiliating and generally useless. I have seen divas in a vocal master class reduce the young singers to a state in which they were incapable of producing a single note. It may be true that sadism is an important element in teaching, but it is better if it is at least partly sublimated and not openly encouraged by being flaunted before an audience.

The greatest teacher does not impose an interpretation but tries to find the way the student wishes to play and to improve the effectiveness of the interpretation. This is psychologically difficult for any teacher, who has naturally developed a set idea of the proper style of playing and of the correct interpretation, and the temptation to force this on every student can be overwhelming. Trying to let the student's personality reveal itself demands a renunciation on the part of the teacher, even sometimes an abdication of taste and of the legitimate prejudices and wisdom of a lifetime. When the student's interpretation and style of playing is not fully developed, this kind of teaching cannot be done in a master class. There the teacher is reduced to commenting on the performance. This can be illuminating for the listeners, who can learn some of the musical issues involved in interpretation and technique, and one hopes that some of it rubs off on the performer. It is true that a very gifted student can take up a simple suggestion and realize it at once, and this imparts a feeling of triumph both to the teacher and the performer. But the ambiguous nature of the master class troubles me: it is an illusion that one is really teaching a single performer instead of casting light on problems of interpretation for a larger group, and it means that one must be more respectful of the pupil's ego than is necessary or even helpful in a private lesson. The indignation that a good teacher may express in private is out of place in a master class. For this reason, I have always made it a policy to allow the student to play all the way through all the movements of a work without interruption. For works like Schumann's *Kreisleriana* or Phantasie in C Major or Beethoven's *Hammerklavier*, this means a performance of more than half an hour. Afterwards, some of the questions raised by the performance can be discussed, and different ideas can be suggested and sometimes realized on the spot, if the student is supple enough and controls his or her nerves. In any case, this will give the student the invaluable experience of playing through the work in a semi-public format, and is a good rehearsal for later recitals or for piano competitions.

The piano competition tends to restrict even further than the conservatory the repertoire of the young pianist, and as the earliest years are the most important, this can become a handicap for life. Since many young pianists start trying for prizes even before leaving the conservatory, their repertory will have to consist in large part of competition war-horses. They will play the same competition pieces over and over again, as many times as possible, limiting the possibilities of broadening their repertory in order to make it possible for their fingers to course automatically through the notes of the familiar work even when they are afflicted with the terrible attacks of nerves that a competition generally brings. It is a common mistake, nevertheless, to think that this kind of repertory will be the most useful for a concert career: the general public does not have the same taste or the same criteria of judgment as a competition jury. The public wants to be excited, dazzled, or moved, and on occasion it does not object to being outraged. The jury is rarely willing to be shocked, and it will too often value simple adequacy over eccentric originality.

An artist must be judged by his greatest achievement. Lord Acton wrote that a criminal is to be judged by his greatest crime. It would not matter if Hitler had been kind to his dog or considerate of his old mother: it is the single worst action that resonates into the future. Similarly, a pianist should be characterized by his finest work: a pianist who on rare occasions gives a masterly performance but plays like a pig most of the time is still a great pianist. From a purely practical point of view, of course, it is worth knowing if the pianist is generally masterly or only from time to time: that helps one to decide whether or not to risk buying a ticket. Nevertheless, the occasional great performance seems to me worth incomparably more than a steady assurance of efficient adequacy. In a competition, however, a pianist who comes up with a performance as bad as some of the ones I have heard from Rudolf Serkin, Vladimir Horowitz, or Artur Rubinstein at their rare worst will not win an important prize.

On one occasion, many years ago at the piano competition at Leeds, I was on the jury: one pianist gave a tremendous showing of himself in the first round, and played very poorly in the second. My feeling was that one splendid performance deserves further hearing, and I lobbied successfully to have him succeed to the next stage. (You are not supposed to lobby on the jury, except in Italy where all the rules go by the board, but it almost always is done.) He was subsequently voted into the final almost unanimously (one member of the jury thought he might not be experienced enough).

On this occasion the jury could not have been more distinguished: on it were, among others, Nadia Boulanger, Rudolf Firkusny, Gina Bachauer, Annie Fischer, Hans Keller, and Sir William Glock (critic, editor, a pupil of Schnabel, and then Comptroller of Music at the BBC—he transformed the musical life of London into a lively international capital). They disagreed radically about almost every contestant (after the first prize was awarded, a couple of members of the jury even made protesting noises to the press). It was Annie Fischer, a pianist for whom I (like almost everybody else) had the utmost admiration, who gave a good mark to the pianist I thought should get another chance; she was rather taken with a good-looking Korean contestant, so I voted for her candidate and she voted for mine. In the next round, I was sitting next to her while the Korean was playing, and she turned to me and said softly: "He isn't very good, is he?" "No," I replied, trying to invest my reply with the proper melancholy.

Local or national pride carries considerable weight in these contests. If a competition is held in Ruritania, the presence of a young Ruritanian pianist among the finalists is assured if there are enough Ruritanian piano teachers on the jury. At Leeds, however, the jury was largely international and Sir William was not guided by chauvinist principles. At the end of the first round, we had, without realizing it, voted out every British candidate. Rudolf Firkusny expressed consternation: "We are in England, after all. We must go over the British pianists and pick the best one for the next round." The other members of the jury pointed out that the rules of voting did not allow this, so the result had to stand.

Perhaps the most revealing incident took place when voting the contestants into the final round after the semifinal (I was not actually present at the final, as I had a recital scheduled elsewhere that evening). One member of the jury—not one I have already listed—proposed that we discuss the various performances we had heard before voting: there were musical matters, she claimed, that could not be resolved simply by voting. Nadia Boulanger was indignant. "If you are interested in music," she said acidly, "you should not come to piano competitions. At competitions you do not discuss; you vote."

Mlle. Boulanger did not, indeed, discuss the contestants, but she had ways of making her opinions known. When she was bored by a performance, she would compose canons. On a large piece of paper she had brought with her, she would rule several five-line staffs, and begin to invent some elaborate counterpoint. The implied comment was far more devastating than any words could have been. A fine performance automatically engages attention and lifts the spirits, but I think that it is not often understood how difficult it is to sit through a mediocre execution without letting one's mind go blank. It is a sad commentary on human nature that a really terrible pianist at these competitions may provide welcome comic relief. The most depressing experience one afternoon at Leeds was three undistinguished performances in a row, all rather similar, of the complete Sonata in F Minor, op. 5, of Brahms.

A few years later I was on the Leeds jury again, and was taken aback when a remarkable young South African pupil of Serkin, Stefan de Groot, was voted out at the end of the first round. Six months later he won first prize at the Van Cliburn contest in Texas. After the first-round results were announced, I apologized to him for the foolishness of the jury, and assured him that those who voted for him had done so with passion. The reason for the lamentable misjudgment was a flawed voting system used that year. We had sixty pianists to listen to, and at the end of the first round we were asked to put down twenty names in no particular order; those with the most votes would go on to the next stage. De Groot was a pianist that one either liked or disliked with great conviction on a first hearing— exactly the kind of pianist who should be listened to again. If you are forced to hear sixty pianists, there will be no more than half a dozen that you want strongly to consider further. The votes were not weighted, so each juror wrote down the five or six names that had taken his or her fancy, and then listed fourteen or fifteen more that seemed least objectionable or most innocuous. This system almost guaranteed that some of the contestants with the most votes in that first round would never get to the third round as their names were set down out of sheer indifference; it also made it certain that some of the most controversial would be eliminated at once. Stefan de Groot was an intelligent and exciting pianist, with a style—like his teacher Serkin's—not to everybody's taste, who would I think have made a brilliant career but killed himself a few short years later while flying a plane.

In my experience the finest pianists, when they are not in their best form, do not give a mediocre or moderately good performance, but tend to produce a disaster or an outrage. I remember, for example, an execution of Beethoven's *Hammerklavier* by Rudolf Serkin in Carnegie Hall, where he missed the difficult left-hand jump at the opening, and, unnerved, from then on never got it right even once on its various returns; when, in the final fugue, he arrived at the unison passage in right-hand octaves and left-hand single notes, he began with the correct A in the left hand but started on G in the right, and, unable to stop himself, played dissonant sevenths throughout the passage; even his phrasing went awry on this occasion. Yet three months before, I had heard him play the same piece to perfection, and he had preceded it with superb renditions of the *Waldstein* and the *Les Adieux*. Interpretive as well as technical catastrophes from the greatest pianists are also possible. As a child, I heard Josef Hoffman play the Nocturne in G Major by Chopin at the racing speed of about 84 to the dotted quarter; I was sitting with a friend of Hoffman's and asked him "Why does he play it at that tempo?" "He can't play it any faster," was the reply. I have heard my favorite pianists perform in a manner that was weird, perverse, inexplicably incompetent, or even absentminded, but I have rarely heard them come up with a performance that was merely all right or just acceptable.

The way a competition is necessarily structured, however, the contestant who plays magnificently once and then very badly in the next round will almost always take second place to one who has performed acceptably each time. This is particularly true of competitions—and it applies to the large majority of them—in which piano teachers make up an important section of the jury. I do not intend this remark as an attack on a noble and underrated profession. A piano teacher, by the rules of the *métier,* is required to react with an indignant protest against an interpretation which is outrageous, unfaithful to the text, or otherwise perverse. A few of the greatest teachers, on the other hand, possess the secret of a sympathetic comprehension of the intentions of the student who has produced a monster. Once, when I refused to play a piece the way my teacher, Hedwig Kanner-Rosenthal, thought it should be done, she said "All right, play it your way, but at least make it sound beautiful," and then she proceeded to help me do just that. Not many teachers, not even some of the finest, would show such a tolerant breadth of spirit. Even more pertinent to the way competitions function is that such indulgence and tolerance for one's own pupils is rarely extended to those of another teacher. There are even cases where a teacher on a jury is unconsciously but clearly out to punish not the contestant, but another teacher or another method of instruction.

I have been on less than a dozen competition juries, so my knowledge here is limited: I almost always turn down invitations to join them. Artur Rubinstein, who had a great and humane wit, was once asked if he listened to other pianists, and replied, "If they play badly, I feel terrible; if they play well, I feel worse." Listening to pianists on the wholesale level of the competition is not more enjoyable than hearing them one by one in recitals. In any case, as far as I can judge, concert pianists are often much less prejudiced than teachers about other pianists: they rarely want to hear an imitation of themselves, they prefer to think they own their performances and have a patent on the style. If I want to hear a piece played my way, I play it myself. From another pianist, I would like something individual that has not occurred to me. Most tolerant of all are composers, who are happy to come upon a new form of interpretation of a familiar piece. They do not demand that the interpretation be traditional or even faithful, only that it be musically effective. And they are sometimes even delighted with a new and unexpected interpretation of one of their own works.

A problem that often arises, is that of the teacher on a jury who has a student or former student in the competition. This problem is strictly insoluble, whatever rules are applied. The more distinguished the teacher, the more likely that he or she will have attracted markedly talented students. The world of good teachers and talented students is not a large one, and its members are likely to come upon each other very frequently on a variety of occasions. (One of the driving forces behind competitions is the teaching profession: a student who wins a prize is most often viewed as a vindication of the method of instruction or of the school. You do not hear it said that such-and-such a pianist won first prize and made a career in spite of the education he received, although it is sometimes the case.) Any attempt to forbid discussion is in vain; you can sense the disapproval or enthusiasm of the colleagues sitting next to you by the way they squirm or breathe ecstatically or by how emphatically they write a large NO! in capital letters next to a candidate's name. In any case, discussion always takes place. On one occasion, a teacher on the jury (whom we will call Ingrid because that is not her name) had a student in the competition (who will be renamed Igor for convenience). Another pianist had played the *Appassionata,* and afterward Ingrid said to me, "One shouldn't use pedal in the second variation of the slow movement."

"Why ever not?" I asked.

"The score reads *senza pedale*," she replied.

"No, it doesn't," I said; "Schnabel's edition reads *senza pedale,* but the original score has no instructions about the pedal there."

"Do you think one should use pedal in the second variation?" Ingrid asked me.

"I don't care as long as it is interesting, moving, and keeps my attention."

That evening I had dinner in a Chinese restaurant with a local professor who had Igor in his composition class. "Ingrid has gone off her head," he told me.

"What do you mean?"

"She just called Igor's parents and left a message: *Tell Igor to use pedal in the 'Appassionata.'*"

Competition rules generally try to eliminate the effects of exaggerated prejudice by striking out the highest mark and the lowest mark given by the jury. This most often cancels the marks I give: either I want to hear a pianist once more very much, in which case I mark 98 out of 100, or I hope never again to have that pleasure, and I put down a number close to zero. On one occasion, this angered a colleague, who was the director of a conservatory, as I had given 05 to a relatively competent but uninteresting performance that seemed to me more like a copy of an interpretation than a personal conception. He felt such a low mark was undeserved. I replied that if it had been an examination for a school diploma, I would have given 78, but if it was for a career, it was the kind of playing that I thought should be banned from a concert hall: it was like selling a fraudulent reproduction in place of an original. He was not convinced by my argument, but it still seems correct to me. A competition should not foster mediocrity. Each contestant should be judged as if decades of performance were lying before every one of them.

Canceling my exaggeratedly high and low marks only worked as long as there was no one else on the jury who thought I had the right idea and applied my system. When that happened, only one of our marks could be removed. It is surely right that our educational institutions should foster a reasonable and sensible style of performance. Nevertheless the tradition of the public concert in Western culture demands that music should be performed not sensibly and reasonably but with enthusiasm. In consequence, the performer should be judged not judiciously but also with enthusiasm.

Together the conservatory and the piano competition, without wishing to do so, foster a limited repertory of relatively familiar works that will be effective in front of a jury. This is not, as I have said, a repertory which is certain to be effective for a public. In addition, this staple repertory hinders the development of the idiosyncratic personality of the young

pianist. The conception or image of individuality is an important ingredient of public success. Both conservatory and competition rightly and necessarily demand an adequate account
of the general repertory. Yet the character and even the style of
a pianist is determined as much by an individual and personal
choice of repertory as by manner of interpretation. Playing
nothing but well-chosen examples of the standard repertory
will do little to set the performer's figure in relief, and very
often success is achieved by a narrow concentration: X will be
known for his Beethoven, Y for his Debussy or Bach, Z for his
Scharwenka or opera transcriptions. This specialization is an
essential and even indispensable part of the process of build-
ing a reputation, although it can eventually become a handicap
if and when you wish to present a broader spectrum of the
music for piano. (There are, of course, competitions which
concentrate entirely on one composer, like Chopin or Bach,
but it is rare that the prizes of these competitions will privilege
an original approach to the composer in question.)

Pianists should, in the best of all possible worlds, play only
the music they love and—this should carry equal weight—to
which they think they can bring an interpretation that is
deeply personal. I have found that many people believe the life
of a pianist is a hedonistic round of international travel—like
"Join the Navy and see the world" but without having to submit to military discipline. On the contrary, no one would
undertake the general and irritating nonsense of concert life if

he or she were willing to consider a different form of existence. Choosing repertory because of commercial pressure or intellectual pressure is, in the end, self-defeating. The only true recompense for the awkward living conditions is that you can play the music you love throughout your life and play it at moments as well as you are able.

How unwise it is to yield to outside pressure may be seen from the field of contemporary music. Competitions and the requirements of a degree in piano will often demand the performance of a contemporary work. Young pianists with little interest in the composers of their own time will often try and find the most anodyne work, thinking that it will bring the most success with an audience. This is generally a commercial misunderstanding. The larger public for the most part is not interested in any contemporary music at all. It is true that they will sit more patiently through a work if it does not assault their ears with the most egregiously disagreeable noise, but that will not be what draws them to the concert hall. They want more Mozart, Bach, Tchaikovsky, Chopin—more of what they already know they like. It is rare that large numbers of the public will be converted and won over to contemporary music or even inspired to buy a ticket by hearing music that does not actively annoy them. On the other hand, at least in centers like New York, San Francisco, London, Paris, and Berlin, pianists and chamber ensembles with a reputation for the contemporary can fill halls by programming the most grating dissonance or the most vacuous minimalism for the devoted and loyal minorities that have developed a taste for them. Playing safe will rarely do anything for a career.

The proliferation of contests has also made life harder for the ambitious. The chambers of commerce of too many towns think that some cultural distinction or benefit to tourism is to be gained by holding a piano competition. A first prize is generally accompanied by a guaranteed series of engagements for one year, and some of the prestige will hang on for another year or two. After that, all too often, the prizewinner is left out in the cold, as if it were necessary to start again from scratch. It is at this point that the formation of an image has to occur, an image that will make the individual pianist appear to be a necessary part of the world of music. Even the cleverest publicist can give nothing more than a limited or temporary help, and the pianist has to call now upon all the resources of his experience of music from the earliest years. The conservatory prepared him for the competitions, and the stylistic demands of the competitions have now become irrelevant. Much of what he had to do to gain the diploma and win the prize has ceased to have any interest. The part of his education that is not suited to his personal view of music has to be cast away like a carapace from an earlier stage of life.

CHAPTER FIVE

CONCERTS

IN TODAY'S WORLD, the white tie and tails of the male performer at an evening concert of classical music is an anomaly. It is not strictly a uniform that characterizes a profession, like those of the soldier or of the railroad conductor, and it is not worn throughout life, like the cloth of the priest, but only for the frequent evening concert. It is rather a sign of gentility. Only on rare occasions is such archaic and uncomfortable dress demanded of others, like the bride and groom and their attendants at a wedding, or the guests at a formal dinner (white tie used to be required at an important banquet at the White House). Musicians are the only ones who regularly have to wear white tie and tails or the slightly less pretentious black tie and tuxedo (at some restaurants, tails are still required of the waiters, but they must wear black tie with them in order not to be confounded with the gentlemen who are there to dine). We ought not, however, to interpret the costume as a claim by musicians to belong to the class of the wealthy or the powerful. Orchestral musicians are still often obliged to wear tails, and, although some of the most famous orchestras now pay very good salaries, no one would think that the players are part of the highest stratum of society, the equal of stockbrokers, lawyers, oil magnates, or football players. Their almost obsolete garments are only a symbol of the dignity of their art and of the ritual solemnity of the event.

Perhaps the dress is a survival from the private concerts given at court that preceded by centuries the institution of the public concert. Even when the public concert was well established and had become the economic pillar of the music business, a great part of nineteenth-century music making was still done in fashionable private houses on occasions when formal dress was required. By this time musicians were marked off from the servant class, but they were still expected to pay for their dinners by performing afterward. Moriz Rosenthal told me that Ferruccio Busoni intensely disliked to be asked to play after dinner. Once, at a banquet, the hostess insisted, and he sat down at the keyboard and performed the last five sonatas of Beethoven without pausing. I asked Rosenthal how Busoni had played, and he replied evasively, "It had been a very heavy dinner." (That was certainly a way for Busoni to affirm the grandeur of his art while subtly admonishing and even punishing the importunate hostess.)

The trend toward less formal wear for piano recitals parallels the movement in present-day churches to hold services in the vernacular in place of an obsolete and unintelligible tongue, or to modernize the language of the prayers,* democratically bringing the clergy closer to the laity. Already several decades ago some pianists began to abandon white tie and tails, opting either for clothes that looked slightly ministerial and priestly or for the kind of business suit traditionally worn for job interviews. It was not only that white tie and tails are awkward and slightly constraining (the most reasonable and comfortable costume for a piano recital would obviously be tennis clothes), they were also seen to be pretentious and, above all, to separate too sharply the pianist from the public. The attempt to diminish the separation is also contemporary with the movement in the theater of avant-garde directors to override the separation between the actors and the spectators. The remoteness of the stage spectacle, the church service, and the concert was seen as a handicap: there was a growing feeling that the priest, the actor, and the musician should be one of us. The concert has, of course, something of both the theatrical action and the religious ritual. Some musicians try to combine both facets. Once, in the green room after a concert, I heard

---

* A ritual, like a church service or a concert, is often valued for its sense of tradition. The poet W. H. Auden left the Church of England when the prayers were modernized, and attended services in the Greek Orthodox Church, happy that he could not understand Greek.

Leonard Bernstein say earnestly to a nun, "I am not a musician, I am really a rabbi."

The separation of artist and performer imposed by the format of the public concert uncovered and made manifest an aspect of Western art music that had remained partially hidden until the public concert became the standard medium for presenting a work of music: that aspect is the independence of the work of music from its social context. This independence may be something of a fiction but it has been part of the established mythology of art since the eighteenth century and even before. The public does not actively participate in the performance of a Beethoven sonata; it does not sing along, nor interrupt with praise or disapproval. It should remain silent and shut off the portable phones, must try not to cough, and ought to avoid rustling the programs or the cellophane wrappings of cough drops. Insisting that the audience be unobtrusive is not a modern development. Already before the institution of the public concert had arrived at its full dominance, artists like the young Mozart playing at court were insolently demanding complete silence from the listeners. As in a dramatic spectacle, the audience breathes silently in the darkness while the performer is bathed in light. During the actual playing, the performer does not betray an awareness of the audience: to do so has the slightly scandalous effect of a breach of decorum (this can be forgiven when it is done ironically). Only when the piece is over may the public manifest its existence and express a collective and noisy opinion. The performer has a name and a personality. The public is anonymous.

For whom does one play? To whom is the performance addressed? These questions are odd because they do not seem at first sight to call forth a useful answer. They are worth asking, however, because they raise a more interesting one: to what extent is the performer aware of the public during the actual playing? This latter question is more pertinent to the pianist than to any other musician. Unlike the string player or the singer, the pianist does not face the listeners while playing; the public exists only in the margins of his sight. Nevertheless, even for the violinist or the soprano, the contrast of the spotlit stage and the lowered lights in the hall make the audience largely an anonymous blur.

This is not merely a fortuitous aspect of the staging but a characteristic of the public concert difficult to eradicate even when the lights in the hall are raised and the performer chats casually with the public. (A number of concert societies ask the artists to talk in a friendly fashion with the public before a group of pieces in the hope of reducing the awesome formality of the occasion.) We can explain the anonymity of the listener most clearly by examining the radical difference between a concert and a lecture. In a lecture, you not only face the listeners, but you are subtly aware of their reactions: are you speaking too rapidly? is the idea you have just presented too complex or subtle and should one repeat it? If you lecture on the same subject for a group of high school students or for a small audience of experts, you will naturally change not only the speed of delivery but the way you make your points.

In a piano recital, on the contrary, the nature of the audience will not—or at any rate, should not—change the way you play the *Appassionata,* a Debussy prelude, or a Stockhausen Klavierstück.* During the actual playing, the performer's sense of the listeners is largely suppressed— except, of course, when they misbehave. We may play different programs for an audience of children and for adults, but we will play a Beethoven sonata for the young exactly as we would play it for the more mature. It would certainly be a breach of artistic integrity to interpret the work one way for an audience of musicologists and another for a lay public. The decision how to play a work is not only theoretically free, but it ought ideally to escape both commercial or intellectual pressures. This is perhaps what is most pernicious about the piano competition: there is almost no way that a competitor can avoid discounting his or her instincts by trying to play a work in the manner most likely to appeal to the jury—that is

---

* There is a story that Liszt was good-humoredly amused when he was reproached for playing Bach in public like a charlatan. He retorted by playing the Bach A Minor Prelude and Fugue as the composer would have played it, then, more personally, as he played it for himself, and, finally, as a charlatan for a grand public—all this while smoking a cigar with great enjoyment. It should be clear that Liszt was delighted to show off his range of performance styles, and that his own whimsical pleasure of the moment had more to do with the way he played than the nature of the listener.

why so many executions at a competition are so well-behaved, sedate, and sedative.

It might seem that the answer to the question "for whom does one play?" is: one plays for oneself. This is misleading. If one plays for oneself, it is unnecessary to do so in public. There are, in fact, three kinds of performance: for oneself, for one or more friends, and for a public. The experience of each is different and individual. Performance for oneself is probative, experimental; playing alone, we are less aware of the passage of time. Playing for friends is framed by conversation; it is part of the occasion, determined by the degree of conviviality, and the music is chosen very often on the spur of the moment to fit the character and the tastes of the listeners. Playing in public not only isolates the pianist: it isolates and objectifies the work of music, and it turns the performance into an object as well. A public performance is irrevocable. In private, one can experiment as one plays, and for friends, one can try the piece again with a different approach. A public performance cannot be withdrawn; it has become an object to be judged.

It is for this reason that the performance in public seems like the natural goal of the aesthetic philosophy that has dominated Western art and music since the eighteenth century. A work of art is supposed to have a value independent of its social function and even of its role in the artist's biography, and the public concert is at once a metaphor for this independence and its demonstration in the economy of modern life.

This independence may be to some extent a fiction, but it is indispensable to our idea of artistic creation. The work of music may be the expression of an individual sensibility, and we may say the same of a performance: but once published, once played, they have become public property. That is why we can maintain that a composer does not always know how best to interpret his own work. His knowledge of the piece may be more intimate at first, but he cannot control future performances, and his opinion of how to play it may be interesting but is not absolutely privileged. We may say that the performer ought to realize the composer's intentions, but we must also admit that very often the composer, the poet, or the visual artist does not fully understand his own intentions*—at least, this is a doctrine of artistic composition that is as old as Plato.

For the modern sensibility, the public performance is the final realization of the work of music. In spite of the rich tradition of private and semiprivate music making in the centuries before our own, it is with the presentation in public that the performance of a work comes completely into its own, attains its full existence. We must rephrase the question "for whom does one play in public?": the odd aesthetic objectivity, real or mythical, demands the form "for what does one play?" One plays for the music.

This may appear a pretentious answer, rather like the

---

* I shall return to this point when we consider the subject of recording.

grand response of Doctor Knock to the reproaches of a colleague in the play *Knock* by Jules Romain. Taking over the
unprofitable medical practice in a small town, Knock, something of an ambitious charlatan, manages to convince almost
the entire population that they are ill and need medical attention, leaving only enough provisionally and temporarily
healthy inhabitants to take care of the sick. In the window of
each invalid there is a night light, and the illumination after
dark is beautifully impressive. The former holder of the practice asks Knock, "Are you not placing the interest of the doctor
above that of the patient?" "There is an interest higher than
both," replies Knock, "the interest of medicine."

Nevertheless, we need to explain why a love of music,
which might seem to be realized very satisfactorily in private,
will induce pianists to submit to the uncomfortable travels, the
depressing hotels, the bemusing receptions, the terror and
nausea of stage fright, and the ever-recurring necessity of persuading the piano technicians to put the mechanism of each
instrument into a more perfect state. We go through all this
because each performance offers a chance to bring a work of
music into something approaching its ideal objective existence. With an ambition that only seems more humble than
the ambition of the composer, the pianist wishes to create a
musical object. It would be wrong, of course, to believe that a
work exists only when it is played. A work has two forms of
being: as a conception and as a realization, and the realization

is only apparently more solid than the conception. Between the public realization and the private, however, it is the public performance that is the more objective, no matter how much of the subjective feeling of the performer goes into it, no matter how spontaneous it seems or is. In one important sense, the public realization is impersonal—that is, it does not matter who listens to it.*

The success of a public performance does not depend on the nature of the public. In private the approval of the connoisseur may have more weight than that of the layman; in public, the ignorant music lover is equal to the expert. A performance that does not please both professionals and laymen is incomplete and has at least partially failed: the best interpretation convinces everyone, even those to whose taste it may be antipathetic. Compelling the unwilling admiration of those musicians and amateurs who have a different perception of the work or style is the greatest triumph. It is true that we may measure the success of a concert by quantity, by the number of people who buy tickets, and that would be an objective economic criterion. For an objective aesthetic criterion, however, one that transcends even individual taste, we need something

---

* I know that Julius Katchen claimed that he always singled out one member of the audience when he first came on the stage, and played the concert directly for her or him. This was only a psychological stimulus, which made a natural confusion between artistic ecstasy and sexual excitement. Katchen would, I think, have been perturbed if the one chosen member of the public had appreciated the performance more than anyone else.

more cogent. The success may properly be determined by the intensity of the attention of the listeners. In winter months any performance of a long work in a concert hall unaccompanied by coughs from the audience must be accorded its due share of admiration. All pianists want applause, but quiet attention is the true tribute.

A cough is the basic sign of inattention. (As far as I know, only in the work of John Cage are incidental noises from the audience woven into the texture of the music.) Musicians never, in my experience, cough when playing in public. Nor do they sneeze, but that may have a different explanation. Stage fright sends a good dose of adrenaline coursing through the veins, and adrenaline is a well-known remedy against nasal congestion. A good, but unfortunately very temporary, cure for hay fever is to play a recital. One might say that stage fright both hampers and helps performance: the fear makes one lose some control, but the adrenaline sends a jolt of energy into the system.

Every musician, I should imagine, has friends, well-meaning or otherwise, who have a genius for increasing stage fright just before a concert. "If you miss the opening jump in the first bar of the *Hammerklavier*," one such asked me, "are you going to repeat the exposition?" (This friend later became a music critic on an important paper.) Sir William Glock was more forthright about the same place: "If you use two hands for the jump," he said to me, "I shall walk out immediately and I shall be sitting in the first row." Best of all was the concertmaster of the orchestra who picked me up at the hotel to take me to play the second concerto of Beethoven: "What I can never understand about soloists," he said, "is how you can remember so many works." Predictably terrified after that, I was convinced throughout that I would forget and come to a dead halt, but got through the piece relatively safely, leaving out only two bars of the left hand in one passage.

How to congratulate the pianist after a concert is also a very specialized technique. Milton Babbitt had developed a large repertoire of the subtly noncommittal: a good sample was "You did it again!" The compliment offered to me by another pianist that perhaps gave me the greatest pleasure was one given after a concert in Paris: "Congratulations on your great success in New York!" (a recital that had been written up with two columns and a picture in *Time* magazine). The greatest formula of all had been developed by Nadia Boulanger, who, I am told, would come backstage, hold your right hand in both of hers, look you straight in the eye, and say, "You know what I think!" (*Vous savez ce que je pense!*)

I must admit an important exception to my claim that an audience does not properly influence an interpretation—but it is simply the presence of an audience, not its character, that comes into play here, and it relates to the essential structure of a piece. We may find in some works a passage that gives a momentary but false impression of coming to an end. This is dangerous, because the listeners prepare themselves for the release of an ending, and become slightly puzzled when the music continues without pause. Such a place, for example, can be found just before the coda of the Adagio of the *Hammerklavier,* where three beautifully simple dominant/tonic cadences in the tonic F-sharp major close the recapitulation of the final theme before the harmony moves swiftly and surprisingly through B minor to G major. I have heard fine executions of this movement briefly marred by the restlessness of the audience at this point, with some embarrassed coughs and uneasy shifting about in the seats. As a matter of principle I am opposed to expressive gestures made by the pianist for visual effect,* but I confess that at such a place it may be advantageous to avoid not only what might seem like a natural *ritardando* but any physical attitude that gives the impression that the performer is relaxing into a final cadence. Even more crucial to a public performance is sustaining the tension rhythmically during a pregnant silence in order to keep the audience from coughing at a dramatic point. One impatient member of the public is enough to spoil a quiet moment. In both these cases, what is necessary is not to fall into any attitude or to make any gesture that suggests that the music comes to a close. I did not always understand this, but I learned it from performing Beethoven's G Major Concerto with Stanislaw Skrowacewski. In this work, the soloist plays the first

---

* I never minded Artur Rubinstein's grand trick of throwing his hands in the air during De Falla's "Fire Dance" from *L'Amor Brujo,* as it was evident that he did this as much for his own athletic enjoyment as for public effect.

phrase quietly, and the orchestra enters after a brief rest of two-and-a-half beats. Skrowacewski asked me not to remove my hands from the keyboard during the short pause and to let them rest silently on the ivories; he found it disturbing when the soloist appears to have finished with the work for a while (which is, however, indeed the case), and I think he was right. The pianist should still imply, even for those who know the music, that the surprising solo entry might continue. This is certainly a part of staging the work for the public. Similarly, it is not effective if the pianist visually anticipates a surprise entrance by hovering nervously over the keys before the moment to start playing finally arrives. Once again it is simply a question of what we might call negative stagecraft, the avoidance of anything visual or aural that gives the dramatic game away.

It is not only by coughing and rattling programs that the audience can be a distraction. Following the score during a performance is perfectly legitimate, and I do not at all mind that some amateurs or students think it worthwhile to keep tabs on my interpretation. It is when they do this in the center of the first row that attracts my attention, so that I am aware of each page turn. This bothers me only because they rarely have the same edition that I have used, and when the page turn occurs in an unaccustomed place, I momentarily lose concentration, wondering if I have made a slip of memory or speculating on which edition they can be looking at. I have on two occasions stopped a performance between the movements to ask a front-row page turner to look for a more distant seat. I give all these details to make the simple point that the less one is aware of the audience, the greater the chance of a deep immersion in the music that results in a more satisfactory performance.

In return, it seems to me that the pianist ought not to distract the audience from the music. There are many pianists who cannot bear the thought that no one is paying any attention to them during the initial orchestral ritornello of a classical concerto. (They are like the opera directors unable to countenance the tradition of playing the overture with the curtain down; they want the public to be aware of their importance from the outset. And until I saw the revival of the original Nijinsky choreography of *Le Sacre du Printemps,* I never realized that the extraordinary opening minutes that represent the coming of the Russian spring were meant to be heard as a prelude in the dark, and was astonished at how much more effective this was than either a concert performance or the stagings of all the later choreographers who raise the curtain before the music begins.) The standard ways the pianist makes the public aware of his or her presence during the introductory orchestral section are raising and lowering the piano seat or fiddling with a handkerchief—the latter method is generally a feminine wile, but Arturo Benedetti Michelangeli had a black handkerchief that he placed in the piano at the opening of a concert and could employ to good purpose. Wiping one's brow after a strenuous passage is inoffensive, but discreetly beating time behind the conductor's back is considered ill-mannered: this is more often a failing of solo violinists than of pianists.

It is true that elaborate gestures while performing not only impress the audience with a sense of drama but also serve to release some of the tension in the pianist, and may act in much the same way as the grunting of tennis players with each stroke (this seems to have been getting louder in recent years). Some pianists and conductors have found it inspiring to sing along with the playing, as if this acted as a guide to their inspiration. Nevertheless the wild gestures and gyrations can also interfere with technical efficiency. This was particularly true of Rudolf Serkin, a pianist whom I admired perhaps above all others when I was sixteen and for some years afterward. I once heard Serkin play Beethoven's Sonata in A Major, op. 101, a work for which he had a special affinity. On this occasion he violently threw his hands high into the air at the *fortissimo* in bar 52 of the march-like scherzo, marked *Lebhaft* and *Marchmässig*, with the result that he hit a formidably disturbing wrong note. This section of the scherzo is repeated at once, and Serkin went through the same acrobatic display, hitting a wrong note once again. After a lyrical trio section, the entire march returns: this time Serkin placed his hands carefully and solidly on the right notes, and they stayed momentarily in place on the keyboard. In spite of my great admiration, I inevitably felt a certain *Schadenfreude*.

Even if the nature of the public should not ideally affect the interpretation, which ought to remain personal and individual, every pianist wishes for the approval that is traditionally manifested by applause. Curiously, the amount and enthusiasm of the applause depend less on the actual performance than on the local traditions and customs of the town in which one is playing. In some cities, the audience loves to applaud: Stuttgart is one such place. At a recital there, I had to play six encores, and the only way to put a stop to the applause was to have the chair before the piano removed. I was naturally pleased, but the next day I was disconcerted to hear a truly awful performance greeted with similar enthusiasm. Professional musicians and connoisseurs tend to forget that even music badly played can sound beautiful and give pleasure.

For some reason, afternoon concerts on weekdays stimulate less excitement than evening affairs. That used to be the case with the Friday afternoon concerts of the New York Philharmonic, which were almost always coolly received. Recitals at the Royal Society in Dublin were traditionally played twice on the same day; the evening audience was cordial while the afternoon concert was attended largely by elderly ladies who applauded politely while wearing mittens. Traditions of applause change from culture to culture. Germans never applaud between the movements of a sonata, or before the end of an act at the opera. Italians traditionally manifested their immediate approval even during the singing, although more recent audiences have been infected by the international preference for silence. I have been told of a performance of *Aida* some years ago at the Baths of Caracalla in Rome before a public of 10,000. After the first aria, "*Celeste Aida*," 9,997 people broke into applause, and three Germans tourists indignantly hissed "Shhh." The attempt to make classical music more awesome by demanding a greater amount of dignified silence has resulted in audiences today being unsure where to applaud. Very often there is no applause or only a timid acknowledgment between several unrelated pieces, as if they were the movements of a sonata. I have even heard that in one town in Switzerland, the conductor had to turn around at the end of a Beethoven symphony and tell the still politely silent public that the work was over.

Applause may be always welcome (except, of course, when it occurs at a virtuoso gesture in the middle of a work at an unresolved and dissonant climax), but it is not always appropriate. Moriz Rosenthal maintained that the custom of applauding only at the end of Schumann's Phantasie in C Major, op. 17 was misguided. There should be enthusiastic applause after the famous technical display at the end of the second movement, he felt, but the end of the slow movement finale should be received in a meditative silence. The most appreciative audience will indeed leave several moments of reflection after this finale. When this happens, I do not know whether to ascribe the respectful silence to the quality of the playing or to the tact and culture of the local public.

We tend to think of all performance today in terms of the public concert; even on records we attempt to suggest the sonority of the concert hall. Gradually over history the recital program developed into a special genre like an individual work of music. Eighteenth-century concert programs were always somewhat slapdash: there was no such thing as a piano recital until much later when it was invented by Liszt in the 1830s. The programs almost always mixed several kinds of music: symphony, concerto, aria, and solo pieces. Not even the integrity of the single work was respected: arias or solo pieces could be interpolated between the movements of a concerto or a symphony. In the mid-nineteenth century, the program of a piano recital was usually a potpourri. It was not thought that the public had much taste for sustained listening to a long work. Even in lieder recitals, a long cycle like Schumann's *Frauenliebe und Leben* or *Dichterliebe* was almost always broken into two or more parts with some solo piano pieces in the middle to ease the strain. Pianists like Hans von Bülow gave a new seriousness to the recital, and either began or enforced the tradition of not pausing between the movements of a Beethoven sonata (Bülow was even reported to have locked the doors to prevent the public from leaving when he conducted Beethoven's Ninth Symphony). I believe, however, that it was in the twentieth century that program-building became an art, so that the whole recital was constructed like a symphony, with an introduction, an earnest and massive central piece before the intermission, a few smaller works that provided a light contrast, and a brilliant finale.

It is true, as I have said, that the nature of the audience will to some extent determine the choice of works—that is, one does not play Bach for an audience that expects to hear Chopin, or Mozart for a society that wants Boulez. Nevertheless, once the nature of the program is set, the public is considered only in an abstract way. The question then becomes only what is the most effective order, and this is answered in much the same way for every type of audience.

We rarely start with the longest work on the program, because there may be some latecomers who will not like to be kept waiting behind the closed doors of the hall for a half hour or more. In my experience it is not wise to put the work most difficult for an audience to comprehend too early in the evening, because it takes some time for the listeners to settle down to sustained listening. On the other hand, too late in the evening their attention may have been frayed. Some exceptionally monumental works present a problem: the fifty-five minutes of Beethoven's *Diabelli* Variations are too long for the first half—listeners will not be ready for so demanding an experience, and it must, I think, be placed at the end; this work should, however, be preceded on the first half of the program by something solidly sustained, as a series of short pieces followed by a theme and thirty-three short variations make a fragmentary impression that is fatiguing. As for the contemporary repertory, in towns that ask for a difficult modern work it is advisable to place this just before the intermission: those who like difficult music will be properly warmed up and receptive, and those who have little taste for it will be happy to have easier fare on the second half of the concert. In this case, the tradition of playing all the music arranged chronologically, which flourished in my childhood, is not helpful: after all, there is no reason for a recital program to retrace the history of music.

I do not much appreciate didactically ordered programs that attempt to demonstrate a thesis (although I have yielded several times to the temptation of placing Elliott Carter's *Night Fantasies* at the end of the first half of a recital and then beginning the second part with Schumann's *Davidsbündlertänze* op. 6, which Carter used as a model, but the contrast of these two works is as remarkable as the affinity, and the combination is musically effective). Some pianists are careful about juxtaposing certain tonalities on the program in the belief that some relationships are less welcome than others. I have qualms about following a work in E-flat major by one in D major, for example, as the second one will sound at first not only less brilliant but also a little flat. I have been told that Wilhelm Backhaus used to play a program all in C-sharp minor. I think I would have found that irritatingly monotonous. Since there are few works for the piano in C-sharp minor, it is easy to reconstruct that program even by guesswork: two preludes and fugues from *The Well-Tempered Klavier,* the *Moonlight* Sonata, Schumann's *Etudes Symphoniques,* a Chopin waltz and a nocturne along with a few mazurkas and the third scherzo, and finally a famous Rachmaninov prelude for an encore (beyond a Haydn sonata and a Brahms intermezzo, there is not much choice left).

Playing in public is not the most nerve-wracking form of performance: playing for one or two friends who are musicians can be even more frightening. I have always marveled at Leopold Godowsky, who was reputed to perform magnificently in private and was greatly admired by other pianists, but was unable to play his best in the concert hall. Nevertheless, playing in public is a special experience, different in kind from any other kind of performance, and it requires getting used to. Acoustics are different, and the ritual of starting a work resembles nothing else. An opening phrase that is not really technically difficult but only a little awkward (like the first five notes of Chopin's Sonata no. 3 in B Minor) can induce an irrational sensation of terror. The first recital of a season after an absence from the stage of a month or two is always particularly uncomfortable. Most difficult is the first performance in public of a piece new to one's repertoire.

These difficulties have been magnified by the decline of concerts in small towns. Before one played a new piece in London, Berlin, or New York, it used to be possible to try out the program for a small audience. (Composers, of course, prefer that a première of their work be held in an important city with proper press coverage.) It is not, as one might think, easier to play in a small town than in a large capital, and the stage-fright that is magnified by playing a new work is more or less the same wherever the recital takes place. But confidence increases naturally with successive performances. The concert series that used to be held in hundreds of small communities is dying out. It is not that the public for them is diminishing, but it has not grown as rapidly as the public for rock concerts, and does not attract investment. Above all, the expenses of travel and publicity have mounted almost catastrophically. Only in large cities is the public concert still a normal constituent of social life.

What makes a concert successful? On the whole, the more famous the pianist the greater the pleasure of the public. This is only fair. In general, the reputation of the finest pianists is well merited. The paradox that needs at least brief explanation is why a mediocre or poor performance by a fine pianist on an off day will receive as much applause as, will be a triumph equal to, the most perfect executions.

We hear for the most part what we expect to hear. This is not as cynical as it may sound. A good deal of the sense and power of a work comes through in an inadequate performance, and even seasoned critics will imagine they have heard what they believed they were going to hear. Several critics of Toscanini, for example, still think that most of his tempi were very fast, although his Wagner was abnormally slow (his *Parsifal* at Bayreuth was the slowest in the history of that house, astonishingly one hour slower than the fastest performance, which was directed by Richard Strauss); his Verdi was generally slower than that of many other conductors, and so was his Brahms, except for the first symphony. When his recording of the four Brahms symphonies was issued at the same time as a set of Bruno Walter's, most critics claimed that Toscanini's tempi were faster than Walter's, although this was quite clearly not the case: his initial tempi were often slower, but they were very steady and, as many musicians know, this can give an illusion of forward movement.

It may seem unjust that a mediocre interpretation by a famous pianist can give as much pleasure as a fine performance by an unknown one, but, as I have said, what makes for success is the intensity of listening, the heightened attention awakened in the public. This attention is accorded in advance to a great reputation; the listeners know that they will be dazzled and moved even before the artist walks out of the wings. They come disposed to admire. It should be admitted that some of the quality of a fine player is detectable in the performance on a bad day, but, more important, the greatness of the music, if it is in a familiar style, will pierce even the fog of an incompetent performance. This is as it should be.* We must grant pianists the same tolerance as politicians. The authority of office will

confer a touch of sense to the language of the most incompetent president or governor, an air of wisdom to the common-
places of the most intellectually inadequate.

---

* A recent Australian pianist captured the sympathy of the general public by his
overcoming a difficult history of mental illness. When he toured the United
States, the reviews of his concerts and recordings were almost universally hos-
tile, and justly so. But the hostility awakened a considerable resentment from
the amateur listeners who had greatly enjoyed the playing. If you knew the
Third Rachmaninov Concerto well, his playing was unacceptable, but if you
had never heard the work, or had listened to it only once or twice before, the
attraction of the music was bound to come through persuasively.

CHAPTER SIX

RECORDING

THE PHYSICAL EXPERIENCE of recording differs in one important way from that of a recital. You begin a concert with the adrenaline of stage fright coursing through your veins but this wears off little by little as you become immersed in the act of performing. What may happen at a recording is the reverse. You start with complete confidence: this is a work you have mastered, and you believe that your interpretation will betray neither the composer's music nor your own sense of style. Listening to a first take, you find it not bad, but you feel you can improve certain details. At a second try, if these details are not exactly what you hoped for, your confidence begins to fray at the edges. What we may call microphone fright appears on the horizon. In a concert, an effect that does not quite come off matters very little if the whole performance has vitality. In a recording, however, a slight slip of memory, a wrong note grazed are an irritant. They are an obstacle to the attempt to forget our own concerns and let the music take over our consciousness.

It is often thought that modern techniques of tape splicing have made recording much easier, but this is only partly true. Before tape, a record lasted at most 4½ minutes. It is not that difficult with music that one knows well to play 4½ minutes with almost perfect accuracy. Rachmaninov was said to walk into a recording studio and refuse to warm up; he would start recording immediately upon taking off his gloves. Then he would play a work as many as sixteen times. Even with all this effort, there are still occasional wrong notes in his recordings (I remember notably a passage in the Scherzo of Chopin's Sonata in B-flat Minor), but his great performances would not be much improved by removing these blemishes.

The move to longer commercial recordings was gradual. The initial leap took place in the early 1950s with the use of vinyl and the first LPs or long-playing records. At first an LP side was limited to a little over 20 minutes, but in time this was increased to 30 and even 32 or 33 minutes. With the longer time, however, there was a danger that the grooves would run into each other: when I recorded Schumann's *Davidsbündlertänze* in 1963, my performance took 33 minutes and 27 seconds, and the producer begged me to remove at least one short repeat (I think in the end that I held fast, and the master disc for production was successfully made only because it was carefully supervised instead of being simply turned over to a machine). The two sides of an LP generally required 60 minutes of music or a little less. In the beginning the LP and vinyl were a boon to smaller record companies: unlike shellac, vinyl was relatively unbreakable, shipping was no longer a problem, and processing the record was cheap once the studio costs were paid and the musicians given their modest stipend. Small companies sprang up for a few years until they were systematically driven out of business by the larger companies who could offer much bigger discounts to the major chains of record stores.

The next leap came with the introduction of the digital recording and the compact disc. This meant both a gain and a loss in reproduction. The digital recording eliminated the tape hiss and the background noise, but it was less sensitive than analog: the human ear can distinguish dynamic nuances that escape the digital system now in use, and the elimination of background noise gave an oddly aseptic quality to records. At first only an hour's worth of music was possible for a CD, but this has been increased to over 80 minutes. (In my experience, however, companies will still schedule the same recording time for 80 minutes that they used to set aside for 60.) Works like Bach's *Art of the Fugue* and Mahler symphonies can now be accommodated on one record. In addition, the discs are much smaller than LPs, and a huge library of music can be housed in a small space. The most important record companies have taken advantage of this for the most part not by recording that area of the classical repertory that remained unavailable (they have left that to some smaller companies who have tried to seize the opportunity), but by transferring the huge backlog of a half-century of analog LPs to the new CDs. As far as the classical repertory is concerned, compared to the magnificently active campaigns of new recordings from the 1930s to the 1980s, the major companies have largely become reprint houses. When the backlist is exhausted, perhaps the making of new records will be invigorated, or perhaps some of the large companies will judge it more expedient to go out of the classical music business altogether. For many it is only an icing of prestige on their real economic activity.

Going from the possibility of recording only 4 1/2 minutes of music to 82 or 83 minutes has changed the process of making records. The technique of splicing has also had an enormous influence. The ability to record for at least half an hour without stopping enables us more easily to achieve a sense of continuity in large works, but at the same time it is more difficult to play 30 minutes completely to our own satisfaction than 4½ minutes. The slight faults that may occur in even the finest executions of a long work often seem relatively unimportant to me (it is never true, of course, that an error is absolutely unimportant), but in today's world of recording the pressure to correct everything is immense: there is always the fear that someone will say "Even with splicing he couldn't get it right." And it is indeed easy to splice. (It was, by the way, even easier to splice the mistakes in the performances on the old piano rolls of the 1920s—all one had to do was paste over the hole that would reproduce the wrong note and punch another hole for the right one. I have always disliked these piano rolls as they never seemed to me to represent the variety of tone quality that I have always admired in the finest playing.)

In fact, the piano is the easiest instrument to splice. The initial impact of even the softest notes on the piano has a percussive accent easily registered by the decibel needle that measures the volume of sound, and easily detectable on the tape. With analog tape recording, splicing a piano recording was almost child's play most of the time. The tape was stopped where one wanted to cut and then moved back and forth by hand until the beginning of the note was clearly heard as a sudden increase in volume like a grunt. The only problem arose when the passage immediately preceding the note on which one wanted to splice was much louder in the performance that was to be substituted: this created an overhang of background resonance at the cut that made it quite clear that some mechanical and artificial trickery was being committed.

During the analog years before the introduction of digital recording, splicing could almost be called a cottage industry. No machines were used except the one that played the tape. Everything else was done by hand, and all the technician needed was a razor blade and a roll of Scotch tape. There was a sophisticated tape machine that would cut the tape for you, but some technicians continued to prefer the hand cut. This cut was generally made on the slant, like the sophisticated cook's way of slicing carrots: in that way minuscule fragments of the sound before and after the note were included on both sides of the splice and assured that the difference between the entering and exiting tapes would be hidden more successfully: cutting by hand meant that the slant could be varied, and provided a more complex mix, but then one needed a precise visual judgment so that the slant was the same on both the entering and exiting tapes. This was a small opportunity for the technician to exercise some virtuosity.

The larger record companies had a rigid hierarchy in allotting the tasks during a recording. There was the producer who sat in judgment, and marked the score indicating the mistakes. He registered the better executions, and kept the log of how many minutes and seconds each take had required, and where it began and ended. There was the sound engineer who placed the microphones and twiddled the dials in order to achieve the balance. Finally, there was the technician who handled the tapes, pushed the buttons to start and stop the machine, and eventually would do what editing was required at the command of the producer. By a curious union regulation of the 1960s in the United States, the tape man was forbidden to know how to read music: that would have given him an unfair advantage over his colleagues. Of course, many of the technicians knew perfectly well how to read music but they could not admit it. That meant that when you wanted the technician to cut the tape at a certain point, you were not allowed to show him the score so that he could see where to make the splice. The tape had to be played, and the technician had to be given a hand signal at the arrival of the note as if he were a musician in an orchestra given the cue for his solo.

This was the system in place for all the years I recorded for the various CBS labels—Epic and Odyssey Records, CBS International, and Columbia Masterworks. When I began, the first records were all made in their official New York studio, which was a large and handsome defrocked church in the low Thirties on the East Side. The acoustics were splendid. However, at one point the wife of one of the directors of Columbia Records decided that it looked rundown and tacky, and ordered some decorative curtains installed on the walls in a few places. The sound immediately deteriorated, became drier, losing resonance and warmth. I blamed this on my playing: after hearing the first takes I said that I evidently could not play the work convincingly, and canceled the session (on only one other occasion did I ever cancel a recording session). When I returned a month later, the curtains had been removed—or at least opened up to reveal the bare and acoustically gratifying plaster walls—and my playing had improved.

The acoustics of any space—studio, concert hall, church,

large private room—pose the fundamental aesthetic problem of recording. We think today of all music as being played in public, as presented to an audience of some considerable size. Records, however, are largely played in more modest venues, privately, for the pleasure of one or two people. The acoustics of the record are therefore always an illusion. What illusion should we settle for? The decision is almost always to give the impression that the sound is being created in a space larger than the average living room. The opera must have the resonance of an opera house, the symphony of a large concert hall. It is rare that a recording of a Haydn symphony makes us think that it is being played in the rooms in which Haydn generally produced these works, rooms in which 150 people would only have been able to fit with considerable crowding. The recording engineer does not ask what the most authentic sound would be for each piece, but—and rightly—what sound will give the most pleasure to modern ears. We are no longer accustomed to an acoustic with too much intimacy. Alone in a room with the record player, we like to imagine that we are a part of the mass audience that we think indispensable to classical music. But we also like to think that we have privileged seats close enough to the performers to give us the extra clarity rarely granted us in public performances.

There used to be a prejudice that music of different styles needed different sorts of resonance—not merely music of different genres (it is reasonable that a symphony should make us believe in a larger space than a string quartet or a song cycle), but that a contemporary piece should have a drier and more acid sound than the standard Romantic works. I experienced the results of this nonsense once with two days of recording for French radio. On the first day I played almost an hour of Schumann, and the quality of the recording seemed reasonable. On the second day, I played Schoenberg's opp. 19 and 25, and listening to the first take I was astonished at the ugly sound, although it was the same studio and the same instrument. "This is the microphone setup for contemporary music," the engineer assured me, but I insisted that the placement of the previous day be restored. I was reminded of Schoenberg's remark, "My music is not modern, just badly played." There was a policy of recording it badly as well: a magnificent performance of Schoenberg's piano music by Edward Steuermann was issued on a record some years ago that made it sound as if it had been played in a confined space like a small bathroom.

Finding the balance between too much resonance and too little is not only difficult, but obstructed by the aesthetic taste of some sound engineers. The first record I made for CBS was Ravel's *Gaspard de la Nuit,* and the sound engineer started by placing one of the microphones so close as to be almost inside the piano. The opening piece, *Ondine,* begins with a soft irregular *tremolo,* representing the shimmering of light on water:

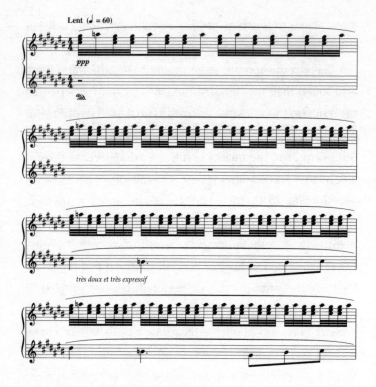

The opening of Ravel's Gaspard de la Nuit

Placing a microphone very close·to the instrument emphasizes the initial percussive impact of each note as it is struck and removes the liquid blending together of the total sonority that was Ravel's clear intention. With the microphone so close to the strings at the upper part of the piano, the sound was considerably more brittle than it was sitting at the keyboard. When I said I thought that the microphone was too close, the sound engineer protested that if it were moved farther away, we would lose fidelity. That was what we wanted, of course: less fidelity. Otherwise the opening page sounded like a finger exercise by Czerny. *Ondine* was meant to be heard in the large space of a concert hall, and demands a considerable amount of room sound. Reluctantly the sound engineer pretended to move the microphone away, and was at last persuaded to make the distance perceptible to eye and ear (an inch can make an extraordinary difference).

Acoustics can radically alter an interpretation—and so they should. It is sometimes mistakenly thought that the more echo or resonance in a hall, the less pedal one should use. The exact opposite is true. Robert Casadesus once pointed out to me that in a resonant hall with a good sound, like Carnegie Hall before the reckless interference with its acoustics of some decades ago, one could play the following octave passage from the end of the first movement of Brahms's Concerto no. 1 in D Minor with the pedal jammed down throughout:

The end of the first movement of Brahms's
Concerto no. 1 in D Minor

In a hall with dry acoustics this would be intolerable. Overpedaling when there is little resonance or echo and therefore too much clarity is disturbing: it blurs the lines and adds unwanted harmonic ambiguities. In a hall with a warm, rich acoustic, the effect of the pedal merely adds to the resonance and gives greater fullness. It must be said certainly that the unorthodox excessive pedaling in the above passage by Brahms works in a good hall only because the dynamic is always *fortissimo*, and each successive note imposes itself with ease and clarity, covering the previous sound. And it should never be attempted in a slightly dry hall like the Academy of Music in Philadelphia (Rudolf Serkin remarked to me about this hall that the sound was good, but it did not help you: it did not, he said, make you sound better than you are).

It is often difficult to judge the acoustics of a hall from the stage. However, the most important part of the acoustics, from the pianist's point of view, is what the piano sounds like while sitting at the keyboard. There are halls where it is possible to feel as if you were playing at home, and this immediately grants a sense of ease to the performance. In halls like Avery Fisher Hall at Lincoln Center when it first opened, the sound while sitting at the keyboard seemed to come from a distance, and this induced a frustrated disquiet, as if a greater energy were always needed to make the intended effect. It is true that the sound in a hall is often radically different from the sound on the stage, but then there is almost nothing one can do about that, and it is dangerous to take that too much into account since the sound can change from one part of the hall to another. The dress circle in Carnegie Hall, for example, is somewhat muffled by comparison with the orchestra and the family circle; the music sounds best if one sits either below or at the top.

At a recording one can at least partially control the

acoustics of the hall by the way the microphones are placed. Situated at a distance, the microphone picks up the ambient sound of the room, and, as I have said, the closer placement registers the instrumental detail, including the extramusical mechanical noises that have nothing to do with the score. One would think that the recording industry would have worked out a standard way of placing a standard number of microphones. This is not the case. One must have faith in the artistry of the sound engineer. Each one seems to have a different system, and a good one will give you the sound you ask for. I have never understood how they do it. There are different kinds of microphones that act with different sensitivity and pick up and emphasize different kinds of sound. I have never wanted to know too much about this: you can tell a good sound engineer what sonority you would like, but it would be a disaster if you had to tell him how to do his job and achieve it. After the crisis of that first recording for CBS, I have never advised or made suggestions to a sound engineer about the placement of his microphones.

Recording a piano in CBS's New York church (they also often recorded in Hollywood where the film industry had attracted a pool of extremely competent musicians), sound engineers used two microphones, one placed at a distance several yards above the piano, the second on the floor at the side close to the back of the instrument. At the EMI studios in London at Abbey Road, when I recorded there in the late

1960s, three microphones were hung fairly high from the ceiling spread out from left to right of the piano. A young reporter from one of the British record magazines came to one of the sessions, saw the three microphones, and said, "Ah, multiple mikes. The American system." When I told him that I had never had more than two microphones in America for a solo piano recording, he refused to believe me: the use of extra mechanical aids could not conform to an Old World tradition.

In some Chopin recordings that I made in Holland in the French Protestant Church in the peaceful red-light district of Amsterdam, I said in surprise to the producer, "You're using six mikes." "Seven," he replied. Along with the records I made with Max Wilcox in the American Academy of Arts and Letters, these were the sessions that produced the most satisfactory piano sound. Max used two omnidirectional microphones, placed not too close to the piano, and managed to capture both clarity and a warm resonance. At all these sites, the music sounded good at the keyboard, and much of what was heard by the pianist could be transferred to the tape with perhaps a little more emphasis on the ambient sonority of the surrounding space.

The large studio at Abbey Road had been altered when I returned there some years later to record the Beethoven Concerto no. 4 in G Major. It had been perfect for chamber works and for a small orchestra, and I had even recorded Elliott Carter's Double Concerto for Harpsichord, Piano and Two Chamber Orchestras in that studio (there were no problems except that the engineer made the harpsichord much louder to balance the piano—"I know that a harpsichord is softer than a piano," the composer complained to me sometime later). Subsequently, however, EMI, who owned the Abbey Road studios, had decided to make it possible to record huge works for symphony and chorus there like Mahler's Eighth Symphony, and added reflecting acoustical material to the walls to give the studio more resonance. The new sound was so live that it was no longer capable of giving a satisfactory balance: a *fortissimo* now bounced back and forth from wall to wall. If one found a satisfactory resonance for a soft passage with enough echo to keep it from being dry, the louder sections became irremediably confused. A proper balance for the loud passages, on the other hand, took away any vibrancy from the softer parts. There was, however, a remedy: the tape had been made with four tracks, to be reduced or "mixed" later to the standard stereo two for issuing the record. One microphone was placed near the strings, one near the wind instruments, a third by the piano, and one high in the air to catch the ambient resonance of the room. It was the fourth microphone that both gave warmth to the softer passages and also left the louder ones with an artificially jumbled sound. When the stereo reduction was made, we did not touch the first three tracks, leaving the dynamics of the instruments exactly as they had been played with no trickery, but we gradually lowered the volume on the fourth track two decibels with each crescendo and raised it back with every *diminuendo* throughout. This manipulation left the performance sounding natural while reducing the interference of the acoustical material that decorated the walls of the studio and disfigured the sound of the music.

The only time that a recording in which I took part was tampered with—that is, where something on the tape was altered by machinery—was in the second of the four pieces of Anton von Webern for cello and piano that I recorded in Hollywood with Gregor Piatigorsky for the album of Webern's complete works planned by Pierre Boulez. Piatigorsky was a very grand figure, generous and hospitable, with a wonderful command of both his instrument and the music, and he had, in fact, given the first performance of these four pieces by Webern (although he confessed to me that at the première he had tried to play from memory and had failed with one of the pieces, more or less reinventing it on the spot). He had, however, recently suffered a spell of mononucleosis and easily became tired. When we did a couple of takes of the second piece, I told him that he was a little late with a *pizzicato sforzando* a few bars after the beginning of the piece.

"Perhaps you are early," he suggested amiably.

"In a way," I replied, "because there is an *accelerando* in the two beats before the *pizzicato,* and you continue in strict time."

"Let us forget about the *accelerando*," he proposed.

"But the piece is only a few seconds long," I objected. "Without the *accelerando* not very much is happening."

"All right," he said grudgingly with a resigned smile, and we tried twice more. The second time the *pizzicato* was right in place, but somewhat soft and a bit timid. I thought it unnecessary to bother him further, but back in New York where the tape was edited, I made a prudent adjustment. The recording had been produced with two tracks: one microphone on the piano, one on the cello (perhaps there was a third track for room sound). We rerecorded the tape with the cello track alone raised two decibels louder until the *pizzicato,* and then quickly lowered the volume of sound right after the *pizzicato* back to the original level. We then spliced the new tape from the *pizzicato* to the end, producing a fine *sforzando* for the cello on that note. I never told Piatigorsky what we had done, but he seemed pleased with the recording.

A record of classical music is supposed to be a reproduction. Like all reproductions it is a substitute for something else, and as a substitute it is thought to be inferior to the real thing, the live performance. This also imposes a moral obligation on the reproduction to be truthful, to represent faithfully the object of which it is only the replacement. At any rate, the foregoing remarks spell out the common view of a classical recording. However, this view carries with it a number of confusions and some obscure paradoxes.

A record of rock music is not a reproduction, but a creation. The realization of a new sound obtainable only by the machinery of recording is a constant ideal in this form of popular music. We may even say that a rock concert is generally a reproduction of a record, and often an inadequate reproduction at that. There is no aesthetic stigma attached in pop music to the use of multiple tracks, echo chambers, splicing, and all possible engineering sleight of hand. Quite the contrary. The recording engineer is expected to have as much ingenuity and imagination as the musicians.

The classical record, however, aspires to be something it is not: a recital, a concert, or a private intimate live performance. Whatever calculation was necessary to make the record is supposed to be concealed, not flaunted. We must pretend that the performance was spontaneous, the music coming straight from the heart of the composer and performer: the recording machines and microphones are only passive registrars of the experience. What we ask from a classical recording is fidelity and authenticity—that is, fidelity to the sound of a performance played as if no recording equipment were present, and authenticity which guarantees that the performance has not been adulterated and deformed in any way. Yet even with the recording of a live concert, these conditions are largely a myth.

To understand how the myth works, it is useful to look at the history of another great art of reproduction, photography. When photography was invented in the second quarter of the nineteenth century, the ambition of the photographer was to be acknowledged not merely as a technician with a mechanical skill but as an artist, the equal of the painter. Photography aspired to the condition of painting—an aspiration that has largely succeeded in the subsequent history of the art, although there is still an uneasy buried feeling among lovers of art that the photographer is really just pushing a button, and that the work of photography is actually produced by the external world or Nature. This leads to the most paradoxical aspect of the aesthetics of photographic reproduction: the more the photographer actively interferes with the simple registration of the landscape, the face, or the object being photographed, the less authentic is the artistic result. We feel that it is somehow cheating to remove the lines from a face or falsify the light of a landscape, and that this cheating would transform photography from an art into a vulgar commercial activity.

There was in the nineteenth century, already at the beginning of photography, much discussion of this problem. Doctoring the negative was thought to be a betrayal of the art by many photographers including the greatest: the photographer must be the humble servant of Nature. There were loopholes, however. At the time when it took long exposures to photograph a cathedral, for example, it was hard to get a satisfactory light both for the general atmosphere and for the necessary clarity of detail. But there was an ingenious way to combine both clarity and softness of atmosphere: the negative would be exposed briefly in bright sunlight, giving sharpness of detail, and then covered up; afterward, when clouds had tempered the harsh brightness, the negative would be exposed again for a longer time to capture the atmosphere. In this fashion, it was only Nature that acted upon the negative, and the photographer merely opened the door to her but did not alter the picture in any way with his own hand, neither obliterating nor adding details.

There was also another way of being true to Nature that brings us even closer to the modern art of recording: we know that in one of the great seascapes of Gustave Le Gray of the 1850s, he made a montage of two negatives, one for the sky and the other for the water, and that enabled him to create a grandiose atmosphere above along with the powerful detail below of the waves and the foam. (Like a good sound engineer, Le Gray hid the fact of the montage, which was only discovered by a later examination.) And so, in spite of the montage, it could be claimed that it was Nature that produced the visual illusion, not the photographer. The photograph was therefore faithful, reproducing the reality of the scene, and authentic, created directly by the landscape itself on the negative without interference. The artistry was dependent paradoxically on the artist's self-effacement, in arranging the process of reproduction so that Nature could appear to speak for herself. The more the photographer humbled himself before the objective reality, not altering it by his own taste, the greater the aesthetic triumph.

We demand the same sort of fidelity and authenticity from our recordings. Whatever montage is employed must remain as inaudible as Le Gray's montage was invisible. Illusion is essential. The record may seem to be a concert, but in fact no record actually sounds like a public recital. A recording claims to be an ideal concert, purified of the distractions and the irrelevant noises of the real thing. Even the recording of a live concert generally involves a degree of manipulation which makes it essentially different from the experience of being there in the hall.

This demand for authenticity explains why splicing a recording presents a moral dilemma, and why the fact of its existence is so often covered up, especially for "live" recording. When Horowitz returned to the concert stage after an absence of so many years, his recital at Carnegie Hall was recorded and issued by Columbia Records. Horowitz announced in an interview that the performance would not be doctored in any way on the record, and a few wrong notes were indeed left in when they were sufficiently prominent to be memorable (nervous after so many years of absence, Horowitz began the recital with a wrong note), but one of the engineers at Columbia told me that they had had particular difficulty splicing the Chopin ballade. This means that Horowitz must have recorded the entire program in the hall before playing it in public.* Before tape splicing came into use, some of Horowitz's most magnificent recordings had an occasional blemish, and in an early recording of the Rachmaninov Piano Concerto no. 3, he inadvertently skips two measures in the finale and merely repeats the place

---

* I was made aware of the practice of cleaning up the recording of a live concert when I played the *Goldberg* Variations of Bach, and it was taped for later broadcast by National Public Radio. After the performance, I was told that if I was dissatisfied with any of the variations, they would retape them and splice them in.

he landed on until the orchestra catches up. In later years, when splicing became routine, he made arbitrary demands. On one occasion, he went to the studio and replayed a few seconds of a Scarlatti Sonata on the studio piano ("It's not worth sending my own piano down for so short a passage," he said), and the producer had to take on the difficult task of making the studio piano replicate the idiosyncratic sound of Horowitz's own instrument. On another occasion a producer at Columbia was seen with one piece of tape around each wrist and another around his neck. "It's the octave passage in the *Black Key* Etude," he explained (a passage which lasts about a second and a half); "Horowitz likes the beginning of one take of the octaves, and the end of another, but they don't fit together. I am trying to find a short piece for the middle." I should imagine that all the takes were pretty good, but the temptation for splicing became neurotically irresistible to some musicians, even many of the finest.

I can understand the moral uneasiness that comes from modern editing practices, but in the end I do not see much difference between splicing out an error and playing a piece sixteen times all the way through until it is satisfactory (the latter method is rather like that of the photographer who takes dozens of pictures hoping that one will turn out well enough to publish). At the beginning of his recording career, Rudolf Serkin took a very austere position: if there was a wrong note at the end of the last movement, he would insist on starting the piece over again with the first movement. As a result, however,

his recordings were somewhat tamer than his best performances which had more vitality and daring. (Similarly,
Horowitz's public performance of Prokofiev's Seventh Sonata
had, at least in my memory, more panache than his recording.)
Serkin must have changed his stand later, because I once saw
the production work sheet of one of his recordings of a single
work, and it had been done in two cities.

I presume that complete authenticity and honesty would
require one to issue only the first take of a piece. A refusal to
allow second attempts may seem a foolish policy, like a rejec-
tion of the retouching of a picture by a painter, or revisions by a
composer or a poet, but the comparison is imperfect. The performance of a work, its realization, is only partially a creation: it
is also an athletic feat, something attempted with the imminent
danger of failure. This is inherent in our idea of performance,
and it is why the use of splicing still seems today like a misde-
meanor. Where recording fundamentally distorts the tradition
of Western music, however, is in the way that it changes the
relation of text to performance: in the past the score was relatively stable,* the performance ephemeral. Before recording
existed, the performance disappeared as it proceeded, the score
remained to be realized again. For this reason, like most performers, I have a particular affection for those recordings of
mine where there was no splicing, and a secret pride for the
ones where the first take could be issued as it stood.

---

* Not as stable as one might think with some composers—Handel and Chopin,
for example—who produced different versions of the same work.

Nevertheless, the obligation of recording is not to demonstrate one's superiority but to make the best record possible. A single wrong note, a memory slip, an awkward phrasing, or briefly miscalculated rhythm at a concert may have little importance, but on a record that will be played many times, it can become a stumbling block: one waits for the fault to come up as one replays the record. That is also why some eccentric performances may be forever enjoyed on disc or tape, but others, delightful at first hearing, can gradually turn into an irritant, a simple oddity that calls attention away from the music. When I was a child, I heard recitals of Artur Schnabel with admiration, and the first time I listened to one of his recordings, I had the same admiration. On successive listenings to the records, however, the occasionally muddied passage-work and, above all, the way he would hurry certain beats for expressive purposes, became harder to support—largely because these eccentric details, convincing at first hearing, lost their power when they became predictable and one waited for them to reappear.

When the work is long, from 12 to 30 minutes, one can be faced with a choice between a passionate rendition with a few regrettable details and a more cautious performance that is correct throughout. To insist on replaying a long work many times starting from the beginning might be considered morally admirable, but it is uneconomic and likely to irritate the producer and the sound engineer. There is also no guarantee that the interpretation will necessarily improve: there is, as I have said, a tension in the recording studio that can become obsessive, and goes contrary to the greater freedom of mood that one finds as a public recital proceeds. I remember recording the Liszt Concerto no. 1 in E-flat and the Chopin Concerto no. 2 in F Minor with John Pritchard and the New Philharmonia, and both the orchestra and I must have been in relatively good form since we finished the two concertos ahead of time, and there was a whole three-hour session left over for which the orchestra had to be paid (the producer hastily hunted up some orchestral music by Mendelssohn so the money would not be wasted). Yet there was one relatively easy passage in the last movement of the Chopin that I suddenly had trouble playing, and I had to do it twelve times while the members of the orchestra sat by and grinned sympathetically.*

True irresponsibility—to the public, to the music, to oneself—is to make an inferior record. There is a real moral problem with splicing only when the result is a performance that lacks unity. I have heard records in which it was clear that there was an inordinate amount of doctoring, and although I could not be sure just where the splices were since they had been well executed, the slight but meaningless wavering of tempo betrayed how much work had been done on the tape. I do not believe a good recording can be made with a mediocre pianist,

---

* Pritchard was wonderful to work with. He always went over the whole concerto before a rehearsal with the orchestra, so there was never any hesitation or discussion about the interpretation while the orchestra was present. He could conduct anything: one of the finest interpreters of Mozart, he did Rachmaninov, Stockhausen, Elliott Carter, and Richard Strauss with equal ease. On the recording we made together, I find my playing of the first movement of the Chopin drily unimaginative, but I am not ashamed of the last two movements, or of the Liszt.

although it might be possible eventually to get all of the right notes. A unity of interpretation requires a large-scale view of the tempo, even when there is a great deal of *rubato* or changes of speed, and a control of tone color to hold the piece together. Some musicians have an incredible mastery of tempo: perhaps the most remarkable in this respect was Toscanini, whose tempi could vary from year to year, but would remain constant from day to day, even down to the *ritardando*s and the *fermata*s (a recording engineer who accompanied the NBC Symphony on a tour of Italy at the end of Toscanini's life told me that the tape of the finale of Beethoven's Seventh Symphony recorded in Turin could be played together with the one from Milan until a few seconds before the end). On the other hand, the lack of a steady tempo is a nuisance in some of the first recordings made of Mozart symphonies on period instruments in the early days of the authenticity movement, before the musicians had found out how to keep these instruments in tune: they had to stop and retune every thirty seconds or so, and the changes of tempo that resulted were oddly irrational.* I am told, it is true, that Glenn

---

* Keeping the piano in tune can be a problem for recording. Strings often go out of tune in a recital, but it is not that noticeable in the vast space of a concert hall, particularly when it is only one of the three strings on a note, although the public may become subliminally aware of it, and blame the somewhat less agreeable tone quality on the performer. It is, however, immediately perceptible in a recording. One string even slightly out of tune stops the recording so that the tuner can take care of it. On one occasion, when I recorded Elliott Carter's Piano Sonata in the hall of the Library of Congress, the instrument refused to stay in tune for more than three minutes at a time. I would record for three minutes and then stop for five while the tuner worked at the piano. This was a good formula for destroying inspiration, and it was impossible to get any momentum for the two long movements. I eventually rerecorded the work in Holland when I had a day left over after doing a Schumann album.

Gould, playing a prelude of Bach that had two different textures (I am not sure which one, but I think it might be the F Minor of the second book of the *Well-Tempered Keyboard*), insisted on making a montage of two performances at different tempos, but this was justifiable because he found the oddity of the combination aesthetically pleasing and the contrast of tempos effective in realizing the different textures; with his interest in recording technique, Gould must also have found it amusing that he could arrive at the result he wanted almost accidentally by splicing two takes together after trying different approaches to the tempo.

Of course, there is always a danger that putting two performances together may bring about an unintentional and unwanted change in mood or atmosphere. It is important to avoid this without sacrificing spontaneity. The easiest way to accomplish this with any work, even a long one, I have found, is to begin by making a first take of the entire work with all its movements, and then listen to it. Traditionally in recording the producer will follow the score as one plays; if there is a mistake, a strange noise or simply something awkward, a minus sign with the number of the take is entered in the score at that place. Normally the movement or parts of the movement are replayed until each minus sign is accompanied by a plus sign with the number of the take that is correct. When each minus has a plus against it, the producer generally feels that everything is done. At this point, however, I always insist on playing the whole work again twice without stopping except to have the tuning briefly checked between performances. The result is two complete performances played with the confidence that there is no longer any cause to worry about the removal of minor errors if splicing is necessary. In most cases, all the material recorded up until then can be dispensed with, and the two complete performances, recorded within a few minutes of each other and relatively similar in style and tempo, are all that is needed. With luck, one of the two will be satisfactory on its own.

Luck does not always hold out. While recording the Beethoven *Hammerklavier* in 1969 at the Abbey Road Studios for an album of the last six sonatas, my best performance was interrupted towards the end of the first movement by some tourists wandering into the studio, perhaps hoping to catch a glimpse of the Beatles. I could never quite recover the momentum, so that, although in the first ten minutes of that movement there are no splices at all, there are four in the last two minutes. The slow movement, which took me twenty minutes back then (I now feel that it should flow a little more dramatically), was a single take. This may give me some personal satisfaction, but there is no reason to think that it is inevitably better than a performance in which some montage has been employed.

In the end, a record is neither a document of a performance, or a simulacrum of a recital, but a presentation of the music to a listener in the privacy of the home. Walter Benjamin was never more wrong than when he said that the cinema was an art for a public in a state of distraction. The true cinephile immerses himself or herself in the screen, as if going back to the womb, even if the adolescent moviegoer prefers to use the experience to make out in the back rows. But, after his death, Benjamin's observation would turn out to apply to television and recordings, the two media which allow the audience to leave the room for a glass of beer or chat with a friend during the less interesting moments. Records have altered the listening habits of the music lover perhaps beyond repair. The intense concentration that the art of music some-times requires has become harder to command, while para-doxically the recording industry moved from short popular classics to the kind of music that required the greatest alertness of the listener.

The most radical change in the history of phonograph records began with Artur Schnabel's recording of all thirty-two sonatas of Beethoven, which he started in 1932, but it is a change as subtle as it is far-reaching, and it seems to me to be little appreciated. Until then, the focus was on the performer; the music was chosen to show off the pianist at his or her best. With the Beethoven sonata project, the emphasis was principal-ly on the music, although Schnabel was considered its greatest exponent. The trend continued some years afterward with the complete recording of the Beethoven string quartets by the Budapest Quartet. This focus on the works gradually changed the face of the industry of classical music, and went on with complete recordings of all the Bach cantatas, all the Haydn symphonies, all the keyboard music of Debussy or Chopin, and so forth. Except for recordings made by famous tenors, bought and listened to by few people principally for the music, the emphasis in classical recording has for the most part recently been on the work, and even more on the composer, with the performer as his most accomplished representative.

For this reason some of the eccentric and ostentatiously personal interpretations by artists of the 1920s and 1930s were no longer felt to be as suitable for records in later decades. The record had become less a register or documentation of a unique performance and more a faithful reflection of the composition. The change in the character of recording has led to the myth that pianism was much more free in the grand old days of the past. A little reflection will make it clear that this is largely untrue: many pianists are pretty freewheeling and even weird today, and many performers of the past played with prim correctness. However, it was not so much the style of pianism that changed as what we consider worth putting on a record today. That is why so many of the most admired recordings of the past can seem at once both breathtaking and knuckleheaded, dazzling and revolting, depending on whether they are listened to either as simply effective performances or as interpretations which carry out the emotional and intellectual possibilities inherent in the composition.

STYLES AND MANNERS

PLAYING THE PIANO was much simpler in the late eighteenth century, fifty years or so after the instrument had been invented. At the time, there were, certainly, different styles of performance and interpretation. For example, Mozart thought Clementi a charlatan, although he admitted that Clementi knew how to play rapid passages in thirds (Mozart solved the problem of his own inferiority in this respect by never writing such passages), and Beethoven found Mozart's playing choppy. Nevertheless, the keyboard repertory was considerably smaller than it is today and much more homogeneous, and the styles of playing must have been relatively similar in most respects. Pianists largely played their own compositions or the works of their immediate contemporaries. Keyboard music by composers of the past, like the works of Domenico Scarlatti and Handel, or of

Johann Sebastian, Carl Philipp Emanuel, or Johann Christian Bach, was almost never played in public by the 1790s, and rarely even in semipublic chamber music gatherings. It was only studied privately for its educational value. At the time, even amateur pianists were expected to be able to produce some original composition and to improvise. Except in conservative England, where there was a society for the performance of ancient music ("ancient" meaning more than thirty years old) and where the Handel oratorios remained an attraction for the general public throughout the latter half of the eighteenth century, music was almost always simply contemporary music.

Today the piano repertoire covers three hundred years. The enlargement of the public repertoire was very gradual. By the 1830s and 1840s, the Beethoven piano sonatas had become standard for serious pianists at least in the semiprivate venue of the salon and later in the increasingly popular institution of the piano recital. At first the only keyboard works of Bach heard in the concert hall were transcriptions for the piano of the virtuoso organ toccatas and fugues. Chopin may have studied the *Well-Tempered Keyboard* all his life, and he warmed up for the rare public recitals he gave in his last years by playing a Bach fugue behind the scenes, but he never played one in public, or even, as far as I know, in the semiprivate salons where he could be heard most often (the only work of Bach he consented to execute in public was one of the concertos for two keyboards).

Two or three concertos of Mozart were occasionally heard by the nineteenth-century public (above all the Concerto in D Minor, K. 466), but his solo piano music rarely appeared in a recital, the piano works of Haydn almost never, and for many decades only the shorter pieces of Schubert were played in concerts along with the *Wanderer* Fantasy which had begun to make its way with a few virtuosos. At the end of the nineteenth century and the beginning of the twentieth, the piano litera-ture of the past that seemed fit for public concerts had grown somewhat and consisted, besides Beethoven, largely of the great Romantic works by Mendelssohn, Schumann, Chopin, Liszt, and their contemporaries. Otherwise the repertoire was still drawn from contemporary composers.

The claim often made that a substantial part of the early keyboard literature was unknown to pianists at the end of the nineteenth century is a fallacy, fostered by the illusion that the performance of music was largely public. I have read some-where that my teacher Moriz Rosenthal never played the Schubert sonatas, but he told me that the last movement of the Sonata in G Major, D. 894, was extremely difficult, so he had at least tried it privately. Pianists with any historical or intellectu-al interest in their art, or, indeed, any curiosity, knew a great deal of music that they never presented to the public. The great historical editions from 1850 to the end of the nineteenth cen-tury had made the complete works of Mozart, J. S. Bach, Handel, Beethoven, Couperin (at least the keyboard works, edited by Brahms and Chrysander), and finally Chopin, Schumann, and Mendelssohn available to anyone who wished to become acquainted with the totality of their output. Haydn remained incomplete until a few years ago, but almost all his piano works could be purchased very early by music lovers, and every one of the 550 Scarlatti sonatas was printed by 1910. Indeed, the piano music of all these composers could be easily found in inexpensive editions disfigured by intrusive fingerings and extra indications of phrasing, pedal, and dynamics recommended by scholars or pianists with scholarly pretensions. For the most part, the intrusive editing was an attempt to make the music of the past agreeable to contemporary taste and apt for teaching purposes, although most of the directions for the pedal and the phrasing would have been found very strange and even unintelligible by the composers of the past. There were honorable exceptions, of course: Hans Bischoff's still useful edition of J. S. Bach's keyboard works occasionally added a few dynamics that would not have made sense on the instruments of the early eighteenth century, but he not only respected the original sources, he also gave invaluable information about the way Bach's contemporaries performed and ornamented the works. Brahms, too, was generally scrupulous in his treatment of the texts of older composers that he prepared for publication (he made a few editorial misjudgments, as who does not?), and he even tried to persuade his fellow editor Chrysander to keep the original seventeenth-century clefs of Couperin, now obsolete—luckily in vain, as this would only have annoyed the purchasers of the publication, who would have found them hard to read. His editions of Chopin's ballades, mazurkas, and sonatas and of Schubert's masses are still among the best we have, although he tinkered in a very few places with the orchestration of the Schubert symphonies.

Selections from the keyboard music of minor seventeenth- and eighteenth-century composers could be found easily in the late nineteenth century, and many of these publications were within the reach of the amateur as well as the professional musician. That most of it was considered inapt for performance in public is not a judgment that we could reasonably quarrel with even if we might deplore it: the largest part—in fact, almost all—of the solo keyboard repertoire for two hands without pedal keyboard* before 1800 was never intended for public performance, certainly not for an audience of more than a dozen or two, and some of it, like *The Well-Tempered Keyboard* and *The Art of the Fugue*, was intensely private, written for solitary playing and meditation. The style of performance of the music of the past, therefore, presented almost no problems in the early twentieth century: played largely in private, it was interpreted more or less as one pleased. The few pianists who were interested in the original manner of performing could try to achieve it to their own satisfaction—or,

---

* In the eighteenth century, not only organs but also many harpsichords had a pedal keyboard.

more reasonably and more likely, combine it with a more up-to-date interpretation.

We divide music today into public music and chamber music, the latter for performance in smaller concert halls. Performance in private at home for the pleasure of the musicians is rarely considered an important facet of music making today, although of course it still takes place in the houses of eccentric amateurs and a few dedicated professionals. In the late eighteenth century, the situation was more complex: there was public music—operas, symphonies, and concertos; chamber music—string quartets and divertimentos for small groups, which could be performed for an invited audience; and *Hausmusik*—music for the home. It is not generally realized today that almost all the solo keyboard music of the eighteenth century was essentially *Hausmusik,* played for oneself or at most for a few friends and guests. During Beethoven's lifetime, only two of his thirty-two piano sonatas were performed in public in the city of Vienna where he lived after the age of twenty. They were conceived principally as chamber music and even, in a number of cases, as *Hausmusik,* although their value for public presentation was quickly understood and exploited after his death.

By the last quarter of the nineteenth century, however, with the increasing commercial success of the public concert, any ambitious new piano music was intended solely for public performance, preferably for an audience large enough to assure a good profit for the presenters. There was, of course, a large body of literature of easy pieces for the modest amateur, but these works for private entertainment or education are generally unassuming and make few claims that will catch the eye of posterity (except for a scholar interested in the sociology of music). It is a paradox, however, that the very late works of Liszt, who had invented the public piano recital and provided the most brilliant examples of virtuosity, were essentially private although sometimes radically innovative, relatively easy, and never played for an audience, remaining unknown until the middle of the twentieth century. It would seem as if, at the end of his life, Liszt was returning to the more private tradition that he knew as a child—and to understand these final works, it should be remembered that Liszt gave up playing in public for money very early, before he was forty.

The late nineteenth- and early twentieth-century works of composers like Balakirev, Brahms, Anton Rubinstein, Albeniz, Chabrier, Smetana, Franck, and so many others are basically public in character, or at least capable of being presented to the public with success. All these composers wrote music that would allow a performer to impress listeners with spectacular virtuosity or—when this was lacking—deep spiritual sensibility. Public music had become not only the dominant, but also the standard, form of composition. A sign of how profoundly the forms of music were determined by public style is the disappearance of original music for four hands, one piano, by the beginning of the twentieth century. There are many works by Mozart and a huge body of compositions by Schubert for this genre, essentially intended for performance at home. By 1900, the production of this kind of music had become negligible: Debussy, for example, wrote only a single mature work for four hands, one piano; Schoenberg, Webern, and Berg produced nothing in this form. Brahms was one of the last important composers to give some thought to this dying form of *Hausmusik,* with the Hungarian Dances and the waltzes for four hands, one keyboard, and his example inspired similar work from his disciple Dvořák.* Otherwise the literature of this kind was restricted to arrangements of public works like symphonies, so that amateurs could get acquainted at home with the music they would hear properly in a large concert hall.†

The ideal virtuoso piece is one that sounds harder than it really is. (Perhaps only Brahms, particularly with his arrangements for two hands of the original four-hand Hungarian Dances, produced display pieces that are considerably harder

---

* One should mention here the splendid four-hand parodies of Wagner operas by Chabrier and Fauré, which are both an homage to Wagner and a joke to amuse one's friends.

† On occasion, a work for one piano four hands could be performed in public. With the elderly Franz Liszt and the young Moriz Rosenthal in the audience, Anton Rubinstein offered Hummel's grand sonata for four hands at a recital in Pressburg (now better known as Bratislava) with the famous piano manufacturer Bösendorfer as his co-performer. Rubinstein played the bass part, and Rosenthal remarked afterwards that the treble was largely inaudible.

to play than they sound—that is the chief reason that these arrangements are almost never attempted in recital, as pianists like to get full credit for their efforts.) The piano music of the eighteenth century was largely directed to the pleasure or the education of the performer, amateur as well as professional; by the end of the nineteenth century, however, it had become almost exclusively the pleasure and the interest of the listener that determined both the form and the style of writing for the piano. Composers could make a living (generally, it must be admitted, a poor one and with little hope or assurance of steady improvement) principally by the sale of sheet music to the amateur, the professional, and the semiprofessional musician, but the music from 1850 to 1910 with any serious claim to attract the interest of posterity is almost always conceived with public performance in mind, and even what survived of the old tradition of *Hausmusik,* those unpretentious works intended only for pianists with limited technical ability, mimics the form and the style of the public compositions. The standard mode of music had become the music written for the public sphere or an imitation of it.

Nevertheless, as the percentage of the population with even modest pretensions to high culture whose members learned to play the piano gradually dwindled, and the number of people that preferred playing records to playing an instrument grew ever larger, the general view of the nature of music began to shift once again. The model venue for listening to music was no longer the public concert hall but had become the living room, the bedroom, or the car—or even, with the possibility of listening to music with the ghettoblaster or the diskman, the street or any form of public transportation; music played in this way is not made public, but on the contrary serves to isolate the individual from the crowd and from the public surrounding. (Music in the elevator or the airplane, intended only to soothe, is a poor substitute for the municipally sponsored, informal, free concerts given in the park that served to cement social relationships and give a musical personality to moments of leisure and to holidays.)

When recordings replaced concerts as the dominant mode of hearing music, our conception of the nature of performance and of music itself was altered. The works of the classical tradition, even those of the fairly recent past, became historical monuments or objects in a museum. A performance was no longer a singular event that would evaporate as it took place but an infinitely repeatable experience; the model execution was no longer one that would dazzle, surprise, or disturb our emotions for the minutes that it takes place, but an ideal rendition of a respected work that could support many rehearings. Recordings profoundly affected our ideas of what would be a legitimate interpretation even in a concert hall: Many of us now listen even to a public performance wondering if we could stand to hear it played that way a second or a tenth time. Above all, the visual aspect of virtuosity was downgraded by recordings, an aspect as important to composers as to pianists even if it had been certainly overdramatized through two centuries by the performers as they threw their hands in the air and tossed their manes; videos of the performance of classical music have never caught on, except for opera, as the visual aspect of a classical concert has always—mistakenly or not—been considered irrelevant. Nevertheless, the long and infamously difficult skips in the Paganini-Liszt *La Campanella* or at the end of the second movement of the Schumann Phantasie op. 17 are not nearly so effective when they are invisible, and the furious octave passages of Rachmaninov's Piano Concerto no. 3 find much of their force dissipated when we cannot see, but only imagine, the physical struggle of the pianist in coping with them. Unseen virtuosity lacks the power of the visible execution, except perhaps to the perception of the professional who, listening to the recording, knows how difficult the work is and wonders cynically and mean-spiritedly how many splices were needed to arrive at the final neat result.

The displacement of interest from the individual performance to the composition that resulted from the increasing popularity of records, particularly those of the increased time-span of the LP and the CD, is a loss as well as a gain. It encourages a certain prudence in the performers, a refusal to improvise or to take chances. It is certainly one of the principal causes of the historically minded authenticity movement, which downgrades the taste of the individual performer and encourages the attempt to reconstruct the sound a composition from the past would have had during the lifetime of the composer. Pianists are urged to become archaeologists, to dig up and restore ancient techniques of performance practice. That this movement gained such strength in the last decades of the twentieth century may seem paradoxical, as it accompanies the blanket permission given in our time to stage directors to run riot in their attempts to modernize eighteenth- and nineteenth-century operas, most often with a total disregard for the stagecraft that was calculated by librettist and composer, and is still necessary if the union of words and music is to make sense.

In the history of the performance of piano literature, however, the obligation of fidelity to a composer's intentions is not by any means a modern invention, even if it has been given additional stimulus by the way we look at the art of music today. The figure of Liszt is instructive in this respect: in many ways the first modern pianist, he was a composer, thinker, and performer with an astonishing range of interests, and he embodied almost all future varieties of pianism. Often inclined to treat the work of another composer as his own property, reformulating and rewriting it as if he were occupying a conquered territory (Chopin was not pleased at hearing one of his works treated this way), he was also capable of the humblest obedience to the text and to the composer's directions, above all when it was a challenge to do so. Berlioz, following the score during a performance that Liszt gave of Beethoven's Sonata in B-flat Major, op. 106, the *Hammerklavier,* gave witness that not one detail was altered, not one indication unobserved, and we know that Liszt in later years criticized one of his students for playing this work at a slower tempo than the metronome marks given by the composer. It was most of all in the performance of Beethoven that absolute fidelity to the text was demanded from a very early date—by the composer himself, in fact, who exploded with rage when his pupil Carl Czerny added a few trills in a performance of his quintet for piano and winds, taking liberties with Beethoven's text that would have been considered not only normal but almost self-effacing by many contemporary performers.

The challenge for the pianist today, however, is increased by the huge growth of the repertoire, encompassing a multiplicity of works and styles that far outweighs anything that Liszt had to face. It is still possible for a pianist to develop an idiosyncratic and highly individual style for a very limited repertoire, but not only would that signal a lack of ambition, it would not protect the individual style of performance from attacks on its adequacy for the chosen repertoire. It is no longer enough to gain a reputation as an interesting interpreter of Chopin, for example, since music lovers now expect some assurance that the interpretation will be not only effective but correct, that it will embody the practices of Chopin's age. This demand is a complex one, since most critics judge the correctness of a style of interpretation either by its resemblance to the way they remember that the music was traditionally played when they were young or by its obedience to the latest and often short-lived theories of historical performance practice. In any case, the pleasure of playing a large variety of music is, in my opinion, one of the best reasons for becoming a pianist and accepting the rigors that the profession entails.

What makes it awkward to deal with the intimidating increase in the choice of repertoire and above all with the variety of styles that this demands is an ingrained prejudice of teachers and critics in favor of a well-established style of playing widely believed to be the only one suitable for public performance. It may make this clearer to consider modern violin technique. Violinists today find it difficult to produce a sound without vibrato, although this would seem to be technically not a very elaborate affair. It is, however, not a simple matter; there is a psychological barrier that must be overcome. Conducting some Purcell with the New York Philharmonic a number of years ago, Pierre Boulez planned to have the strings play without vibrato, as the continuous use of vibrato is assumed to be a relatively recent development in the history of string playing—it helps to project the sound in a large hall. He finally gave up the idea: there was no time to rehearse it, he said. There is indeed a small specifically technical problem: when playing without vibrato, a violinist must be sure to start each pitch in the exact center of the note, as there is no longer the possibility of an immediate but inaudible adjustment facilitated by the use of vibrato. Above all, however, the difficulty is psychological, a belief that a sonority without vibrato would be unacceptable or unpleasing to a modern audience.

In the same way, for pianists, there are certain specific but limited kinds of sonority and also certain aspects of what has traditionally been accepted as expressive playing that are thought to be indispensable for any public presentation. Playing with what is called a beautiful sound is supposed to be essential: what this generally means is by common consent restricted to a style of execution in which the melodic voice is set slightly in relief over the accompaniment, violently contrasting accents are avoided, and the pedal is used throughout but with discretion, avoiding any suggestion either of harmonic blur or of a dry sonority. This beautiful sound is international, although modified slightly in different national cultures. In much French pianism, for example, the melody is not quite so prominently set over the other voices as in the Viennese school: the latter style is best characterized by Busoni's remark, "Any melody worth playing should be played *mezzo-forte.*" I was raised in the latter school; therefore it still seems fundamental to me (although my teachers were the good Viennese who left their native city in 1938). Busoni's recommendation has a lot of sense, but I recognize that it can occasionally do irreparable harm to music that strays far from the Viennese tradition, and is often enough disastrous even to much of the Viennese and Central European repertoire. It discourages a variety of individual approaches to the large piano literature, and prevents both any reexamination of the evidence for the different performance practice of the past and any new effort to adapt the music to the conditions of modern musical life.

Fashionable tics of expression are still more troubling. In the twentieth century, there developed in Vienna a mechanical habit of beginning each phrase slightly under tempo, accelerating as the phrase proceeded, and then slowing down at the end. The continuous rise and fall of tempo articulated the music monotonously rather like a string of sausages. The habit seems to me even more irritating than a rigidly metronomic performance, and it is equally mechanical.

Also from Vienna, I believe, has come the recent fashion for reviving the old habit of playing with the hands not together—that is, playing the left hand before the right. In the eighteenth century, this was called *rubato* (or *temps dérobé*), and considered an expressive ornament. (When Chopin said that in *rubato* the left hand plays strictly and the right hand more freely, this is the kind of *rubato* he was indicating here, although there are other meanings to the term and other kinds of *rubato* in Chopin.) When he was in Italy, Mozart wrote to his father that the Italians were very astonished when they heard him play *rubato* so we may assume that it was essentially at that time a Central European technique. A glance at Mozart's Rondo in A

Minor will show that he used it to decorate the return of a theme. This kind of *rubato* was rare in the playing of Horowitz and Schnabel, and almost completely absent from the playing of Artur Rubinstein, Rudolf Serkin, and most of their contemporaries. The claim sometimes made that all pianists in the first quarter of the twentieth century played consistently with this sort of *rubato* and continuously delayed the melody notes in the right hand is manifestly untrue, as any extensive listening to old recordings will show. It was not systematically but sparingly employed by the finest artists.

There were indeed a few pianists who abused the device, in particular Paderewski, in whose hands it was almost monotonously omnipresent (he had studied in Vienna with Leschetizky). An excellent American pianist, Harold Bauer, employed it most of the time: in his beautiful recording of Schumann's *Des Abends* his hands almost never coincide, and in this piece, once you get used to it, the device gives great fluidity to the movement. Other pianists used it more sparingly and that economy certainly corresponds to the older tradition in which the *rubato* added expression either to a contrasting or to a recurring texture. In Josef Hoffman's recording of Chopin's Waltz in C-sharp Minor, made for Brunswick records in 1924, his hands stay together throughout the outer framing sections, but when the new lyrical theme of the central section in D-flat major arrives, his right hand is delicately and unostentatiously—almost imperceptibly, in fact—delayed on every beat.

The attempt to revive the technique is very recent, wide-spread if not universal, and some pianists use it relentlessly—not only young pianists, but a few whose careers are already on the edge of middle age. The trouble with any systematic employment of an expressive device is that it ends up as a cheap way of persuading the listener that one is playing with deep feeling and sensibility, with the expression smeared like butter indiscriminately over every phrase of the work. Instead of stimulating a rethinking of the expression of each work, the fashionable *rubato* of playing with the hands apart has become a mechanism that substitutes itself for expression and replaces interpretation. In a similar fashion, the insistence on what is thought to be a beautiful tone quality systematically taught in most music schools ends up by blocking any essay at coming to terms with the styles of different periods and any consideration of how works written at a time that pianos had a different sonority and tone quality can be made effective on the modern piano without destroying their individuality. It ought to be evident that it is absurd to play Bach with the same tone quality as Mozart, or Chopin or Bartók, but that is what is so often encouraged, not only by academic training but even by critical taste.

Both the uncritical acceptance and the dogmatic revival of a tradition can be deadening: a tradition prolonged is uncon-sciously altered and hardened as it comes down to us, becom-ing rigid and preventing the free play of imagination; an old tradition revived is often misunderstood and misapplied with a disastrous enthusiasm—a recent example is the continuous tiny inflation-deflation or crescendo-decrescendo, dubbed "hairpin dynamics" and plastered two decades ago on every note in a piece from the Baroque period. Simply imitating the finest performers of the past when they have been document-ed by recordings is a bad policy; they themselves did not arrive at excellence by aping their predecessors—on the contrary, the reaction of each generation to the one before is commonly profound. There is certainly no reason to think that the pupil of a pupil of a pupil of Beethoven reproduces anything like the way Beethoven played. Basically, our problem is to rid our-selves of complacency and avoid the two complementary forms of subservience: an exaggerated obedience to what is considered academically correct or fashionable, and a self-indulgent and frivolous confidence in our own ego. A perfor-mance ought always to give the impression of a fresh contact with the music, an original approach that respects the work. "I have never heard that music played that way before" is not a compliment if the performance does not reveal an aspect of the work that we feel was already there but unnoticed before. We all pay lip service to the ideal that a good performance must be an illuminating renewal of even the most familiar work, but how to achieve that renewal cannot be reduced to a system and will differ from one pianist to another.

One method of arriving at an original and yet responsible

approach has been found useful, although it may be overvalued: that is to return to the sources, to abandon the traditional editions and look instead at the manuscripts and the original printings. This may be stimulating: it can give the pianist the impression of making a more direct contact with the composer. We think we have entered the creative mind as we study the eccentricities of the handwriting, observe the hesitations and the slips of the pen. We become part of the age in which the work first appeared as we look at the unfamiliar engraving, the different form of notation, the obsolete ways of indicating pedal and accents. The alien handwriting and notation can have an extraordinary effect of suggestion; we start to notice details of the text that have escaped us, and which may even have escaped everyone else until we came along—or so we might think until we become better acquainted with the words and performances of those that came before. This does not detract from the stimulus afforded us by the original sources. They can make us see the music in a new light.

This kind of scholarship breeds confidence, makes us think we are experts, and may inspire a new interpretation. However, we must remind ourselves that some of the finest performances of the past have been based on faulty editions and faulty premises. Schnabel's fine performances of Beethoven are not invalidated by his mistaken belief that Beethoven's indications of phrasing were erratic and unsystematic. Even today almost all editions of Schumann are very bad, but that has not prevented many great interpretations. A satisfying performance of Bach does not depend as much as scholars might like to believe on the correction of the multiple errors of transcription of his manuscripts or on an absolutely faithful reconstruction of the way his music was performed during his lifetime. The music has survived an incorrect text and a mistaken idea of the notation for centuries. It would be true to say that, in the end, it is not so much the composer or the music that benefits from the study of manuscript and original edition as the performer. Inspired by the belief that this study brings us closer to the composer's mind and spirit, the pianist may be forced into a fruitful rethinking of the music. The belief may be too often mistaken, but the illusion of coming into direct contact with the past is intoxicating and persuasive, and it can result in an interpretation that carries conviction. Sometimes confidence is all that is needed.

The immense piano repertoire* now considered viable for public performance starts with Johann Sebastian Bach, just as so much piano pedagogy begins with his works. In our time, the tradition of Bach on the piano finds itself in disarray. Fifty years ago there was a standard way of playing Bach on mod-

---

* I shall not try to mention every composer who has made a great contribution to the literature of the piano, but only those few who have made an important and lasting innovation to the technique of playing or to the way the sonority of the instrument is exploited.

ern instruments that, whatever its merits and defects, is no longer acceptable. Perhaps it raised few problems at that time because it was considered wrong to play it on the piano at all. The "authenticity" movement started with Bach; distinguished harpsichordists like Wanda Landowska and Ralph Kirkpatrick were active in the 1940s, and it was generally felt to be immoral to play the keyboard works on anything except a harpsichord (the clavichord was held in less esteem simply because it was almost inaudible when played in a hall of even very moderate size). In the following years, through the influence of Glenn Gould and other pianists, Bach became once again respectable on a Steinway. Mozart, however, took his place in the authenticity movement, and for a few decades his works were judged unacceptable on modern pianos. Towards the end of the twentieth century Chopin and Schumann became the fashionable candidates for the project of reviving the older instruments, as the best known conductors of Mozart on eighteenth-century instruments began to receive more invitations to direct the larger established symphony orchestras and partly renounced the antiquarian ideology. In the last few months, historicist performance practice has abandoned the Romantics, pushing them aside to make way for playing Verdi on ancient instruments.

In the 1940s and 1950s the academic way of playing Bach by those who persevered with him on the piano in the teeth of the propaganda for the harpsichord felt that the correct approach was one of sober restraint, and this approach was sanctified by the teaching in the academy. In playing a fugue, it was always thought to be important to bring out every appearance of the theme with the other voices held to a subsidiary dynamic level: in this way a fugue was realized as a series of *mezzo forte* entries of the theme extracted like plums from the rest of the texture, which formed a sort of background cake of neutral flavor. This method did not benefit the fugues of Bach, in which, after all, the principal interest lies not in the main theme but in the way the theme combines with the interesting motifs of the other voices, themselves often derived from the theme itself.

Once in Paris in the 1950s I heard a performance by the English pianist Solomon of a fugue from the *Well-Tempered Keyboard* that was a revelation: it was the C minor fugue from the second book, and the listener was convinced that Solomon brought nothing out and that nevertheless one could hear every note in each voice. The tone quality was the simple, unified *cantabile* considered appropriate for Bach at the time, the tempo a calm, reflective movement, and the balance of the sonorities was so exquisite that the performance, stylistically correct or not, was deeply moving. I have always had a great admiration for an artist who appears to do nothing while achieving everything.

The muddled thinking on the performance of Bach on modern instruments can be seen in the preface to Ralph

Kirkpatrick's remarkably satisfactory edition of the *Goldberg* Variations (a work written specifically for a double keyboard harpsichord). He recommended sternly that the pianist use the pedal only for special effects of sonority but never to achieve a legato, which had to be accomplished entirely by the fingering. Kirkpatrick evidently felt that it was cheating to use the pedal for a legato, since there is no pedal for that purpose on a harpsichord, and he must have believed that it gave the pianist an unfair advantage. Oddly it did not seem to him reprehensible to use the pedal for effects of tone color which were certainly inconceivable for the composer and stylistically anachronistic. Nor did he reflect that fingering on the piano must be different from that on the harpsichord, as on the piano the fingering will affect the tone color which is uniform on the harpsichord whatever fingers are used. An awkward fingering on the piano might alter the accent or make an absolutely even quality impossible, but no such problem exists for the harpsichordist. Kirkpatrick's irrational recommendation demonstrates the extent to which a keyboard player is dominated by the purely physical or muscular experience of pushing down the keys, and how this will affect a view of the music and its interpretation. For Kirkpatrick, his experience of achieving a legato by fingering alone was paramount, and he was even willing to abandon the aesthetic of a reasonably authentic sound in order to retain the equally authentic physical sensation.

Today with no universally accepted standard, with neither

authentic sound nor the sober academic *cantabile* able to command allegiance or conviction, performances of Bach on the modern piano range from the wildly eccentric, successful only if the pianist's sensibility is exceptionally interesting, to a repressed unvarying drive through the piece that sounds like the computer-generated music used on Japanese telephone machines, produced to keep you patiently on the line while you wait for your party to acknowledge the connection.

What makes playing Bach on the keyboard even more of a problem is that almost none of his keyboard music for two hands without pedal was intended for public presentation. Most of the great works were educational: even the single work which makes perhaps the greatest virtuoso effect in a public concert, the thirty *Goldberg* Variations, was probably never played in its entirety even for a small audience of a dozen people before 1810, when E. T. A. Hoffmann described such a modest performance in a salon (people began to leave by the fourth variation, and only one listener remained at the end). Playing Bach for oneself or for a friend or pupil looking at the score (the way the *Art of Fugue* or the *Well-Tempered Keyboard* or the *Goldberg* Variations would have been played before 1770) raised few problems; nothing had to be brought out, the harpsichordist (or a pianist on a Silbermann pianoforte, the instrument manufactured by a friend of Bach) experienced the different voices through the movement of the hands, the listener saw the score and followed all the contrapuntal complexity disentangling the sound visually while listening. Bach's art did not depend on hearing the different voices and separating them in the mind, but on appreciating the way what was separate on paper blended into a wonderful whole.

In our time, performing Bach in public as if one were alone or with a friend or two looking on is a self-defeating project; it would be an exercise in ideology run berserk. Playing in public means publishing the music, making it available, not simply audible, to the public. An austere attempt to restrict oneself in a concert hall or on a recording to those limited means of articulating the music that the composer himself had at hand will appear equally futile when we reflect that for the great keyboard works of Bach there was in fact no contemporary public, and he would never have had to make use of any means to clarify his work: the music would never have needed that kind of help. In our time, however, in a concert hall or on a record for a public that is not expected to look at the score, it is only sensible and rational to try to make both the separate lines and the extraordinary way they merge aurally perceptible and understandable for the listeners in a manner that neither insults their intelligence and the music itself by dissecting the score with an overtly didactic condescension nor leaves them in the dark about the wonderful artistry of the work by settling simply for a generally agreeable impression. I do not know of any single method to solve this problem. Not all of the details of a work of Bach can be made intelligible to every listener, and one needs an individual approach to each piece, an individual decision on what can be set in relief and how much tact has to be employed to do so.

The musicians of the early eighteenth century, amateur as well as professional, were content with a single dynamic level for long stretches that irritates the taste of musicians and music lovers today. It was difficult to alter the registration and, therefore, the dynamics, during a rapid piece on a harpsichord because on most instruments the changes were made not with convenient pedals, as on modern harpsichords, but with stops worked by hand. If you had an expensive harpsichord with two keyboards, you could shift from one to the other, but most harpsichords had only one. Not until the last quarter of the eighteenth century did a greater variety of dynamic levels become essential to general taste. Most interpretations of Bach in our time cater to the modern preference for variety by adding different dynamic effects, playing some passages delicately, others with more dramatic force, and most pianists find this avoidance of monotony absolutely essential. Unfortunately there are few pieces of Bach that were planned to accommodate these changes of touch and levels of sonority. Consequently in most cases they are imposed arbitrarily on the musical structure without regard to the original character. Sometimes they do not work too badly; at other times the musical structure and the dynamics seem to be on different wave lengths. All told, the performance of many of the works of Bach today seems to raise problems that have very little to do with the music itself, but only with the task of holding on to the audience's attention.*

The few examples of fingering that have come down to us from Bach himself show that his style of playing was considerably more detached and highly articulated than the one we are used to today. It is also evident from contemporary sources that Mozart's playing was more articulated than we might expect, and after his death there was a reaction to this detached style and an attempt to give piano technique a greater continuity. Beethoven may have played Mozart's Concerto in D Minor, K. 466, since he wrote cadenzas for it, and he certainly played with a more emphasized *legato* and *cantabile* than Mozart. Are we sure that Mozart's articulation was more suitable for a work as revolutionary as this concerto? We may ask ourselves whether the greater desire for continuity and a *cantabile* style that came with Beethoven's generation were not to a great extent inspired by Mozart's innovations in composition. Is it not possible that Mozart's successors had developed a more satisfactory way of realizing his scores? The nineteenth-century editions of Mozart, even the critical edition published by

---

* The early eighteenth-century music lover could also stand a series of pieces in the same key with no harmonic variety. By the fourth quarter of the century, the public wanted more harmonic variety. In suites by Bach or Handel, all the dances are in the same key. When Mozart started a suite in the Baroque style for piano, the overture was in C major, the fugue in A minor, the allemande in C minor, and the courante in E flat (after which he got tired of the pastiche and abandoned it, although the last two dances are wonderful pieces). His aborted attempt shows how much taste had changed.

Breitkopf & Härtel, added many indications of *legato* over Mozart's passage-work that are certainly inauthentic. The style of playing the piano changed very rapidly, and it would be an incautious judgment that assumed that it always changed for the worse. My own taste goes to a performance that preserves the detached articulation intended by Mozart and Haydn, and I think that the quality of the music is enhanced by this fidelity to the phrasing, but I am not willing to dismiss a more modern *legato* out of hand; Mozart's music supports a range of performance styles. I prefer a correct execution to an unfaithful one, but I would choose the inspired performance over the pedestrian one.

Mozart gave his approval to a piano with good pedals, but there is not a single indication of how to use the pedal in all of Mozart's works. Walter Gieseking insisted that one should never use pedal in Mozart as he had examined one of Mozart's instruments and had found no pedals on it. Paul Badura-Skoda remarked that it was a pity Gieseking was so tall; if he could have stooped down a little further, he would have noticed that the pedals on Mozart's instrument were operated by the pianist's knees. It still remains doubtful how Mozart would have used the pedal and where, but it is absolutely certain that he did not employ it as Schumann did, or as almost every pianist who performs Mozart does today, even many of those who play eighteenth-century instruments or replicas. The few indications of pedal in Haydn and the more numerous ones in Beethoven will show us that the pedal at that time was a special effect, a tone color contrasting with the more normal dry sound.

This poses a dilemma. It is all very well to decide to use the pedal exactly as Mozart was likely to use it—that is, only in selected passages and as a contrasting color. Even if we use Mozart's piano, however, we do not play in his halls, much smaller than would be economically advisable today, and we do not play for his audience. Historical purity is not the most important goal of a performance, particularly when we consider that we can never be sure that we are getting it right. The various aspects of music are too closely entwined: using the pedal as the composer intended is meaningless unless the phrasing, the dynamics and the acoustics are also correct, since the pedal will need to be altered if the phrasing is changed, the dynamics ill-interpreted, or the acoustics too dry. And of course it is better to get all the aspects wrong if the performance is thereby made more effective, although my own prejudice, as I said, lies with the interpretation that respects the composer's directions with absolute fidelity and yet with imagination—neither is worth much without the other. By the twentieth century, recordings can document composers' intentions for us, and when the composer is also a great performer, his execution may be considered privileged. The record that Rachmaninov made of his Piano Concerto no. 3 with the Philadelphia Orchestra makes every other pianist's performance sound less effective and more effeminate or more vulgar, and presents a model for execution that pianists would be well advised to imitate. That advantage is not given us with Mozart.

Keyboard technique changed radically between Bach and Mozart, as the style demanded a greater dynamic contrast and more dynamic nuances. Most of the music of Mozart was always meant for an audience, even if it was sometimes a small private one. On a modern piano the difficulty with his work lies principally in finding the balance between treble and bass, as the bass register on the concert grand today has become abnormally heavy. That means that we must play the bass lightly, but we must not appear to be holding back as that will weaken the dramatic effect. No composer has ever combined the extremes of power and grace with the success of Mozart. It seems to me that the major fault of most performances of his work is that musicians attempt only too obviously to restrain the dramatic force so often called for by the music in order to realize its extraordinary grace. For example, the detestable but widespread habit of playing the final accented notes of a phrase in Mozart with exaggerated delicacy, withholding the clearly implied and often explicitly directed *forte,* attenuates the power and makes the music coy when it was clearly supposed to be commanding and authoritative. Perhaps the root of the problem lies in trying to make Mozart sound what is vulgarly presumed to be typically eighteenth century (this was the criticism that Bernard Shaw made of the performances of

Mozart by the young Thomas Beecham). The difficulty of realizing grace and power simultaneously is exacerbated when the music is played on the more brilliant modern instruments: where Mozart wrote *fortissimo,* he did not indicate a specific level of decibels; he was simply asking the musicians to play with great force. It is that force that we are obliged to reproduce, not the volume level of the eighteenth-century instruments: in any case, when Mozart is heard in the modern concert hall, the original volume has become completely irrelevant, but it is still the drama that counts. Another fallacy of the study of performance practice is the belief that we should arrive at the proper sound of an eighteenth-century work by calculating the average sound it might have had at the time; since a symphony of Mozart could be performed during his lifetime with a force of anywhere between four and forty violins, this average is meaningless. Each work demands an individual interpretation, and there is no reason to think that there is a unique form of realization even for a single work.

The range of tone color in piano music was considerably enlarged by Beethoven, but it is often forgotten that he continued to use Mozartean textures and sonorities at times for contrast and even simply for their intrinsic interest. He wanted a greater use of *legato* than Mozart, but often called for the slightly detached and old-fashioned *non legato* touch. Beethoven seems never to have thrown away a scrap of paper, and at the end of his life he revived motifs that he had invented thirty years earlier; he also never relinquished any part of the tradition that he had absorbed when a child; he added to it and magnified it in ways that startled and even enraged his contemporaries, although most musicians and music lovers ended by being converted to his innovations. Only once in all of Mozart's piano music does one find a *pianissimo* next to a *fortissimo* (in the development section of the Sonata in A Minor, K. 310), but this strong opposition is demanded frequently by Beethoven from the beginning of his career. His use of tempo marks was very similar to Haydn's and Mozart's, although more nuanced, and he wanted a much more supple interpretation of tempo (although the belief of some interpreters that every theme in a work of Beethoven must be played at a different tempo is a perverse misunderstanding). His metronome marks, he wrote to a publisher, are only valid for the opening bars because one cannot put a measure to sentiment, but he did not intend them to be completely irrelevant for the movement as a whole, merely interpreted with tact. He often directs a passage to be played *espressivo*, a term never found in Mozart, and it is clear that he meant by that term a free interpretation of the tempo: at two points of the *Prestissimo* movement of the Sonata in E Major, op. 109, the indication *un poco espressivo* is followed eight bars later by the direction *a tempo*. Pianists often interpret this direction of *un poco espressivo* (when they pay attention to it) as a slight but gradual slowing-down or *ritardando*, but it should be an immediate but not exaggerated change or *ritenuto*.* The greater range of Beethoven's style, which sometimes lacks the intensity of grace found in Mozart's, often requires not only a less strict tempo but also a far greater variety of positions of the hand in order to execute the different kinds of touch needed to realize the new tone colors. I find that a Beethoven *legato* often benefits from being rendered by overlapping the individual notes, while Mozart needs a clearer articulation. This classical transparency of articulation, however, still holds sway in Beethoven, and musicians today often do not realize the rule of eighteenth-century notation still valid in Beethoven that a note before a rest was generally played with less than its written value, never with more.

It is not until Liszt, Chopin, and Schumann that we reach modern pianism. Almost all modern piano pedagogy is based upon the styles they and their contemporaries created. The fluidity of piano sonority, the blending together of successive harmonies, the *chiaroscuro* of the finest playing comes from their work and from their less distinguished contemporaries. The three great figures were different in many ways. Their use of the pedal is a good example. Schumann's use was heavy and almost unremitting; the dry sound without pedal in his work is always an unusual effect, generally singled out for special mention as in *Eusebius,* the self-portrait of the introvert side of

---

* *Every espressivo* in the Sonata in C Minor, op. 111 is accompanied by *rit.*— that is *ritenuto* or *ritenente.*

his personality in *Carnaval*. There the quiet outer sections must be played absolutely without pedal in order to realize the sense of severely repressed emotion, which breaks out in the center with a grand sonority swamped with pedal, only to be held back again at the end. (This passage is historically instructive: the pedaled sonority is the most effective one in a public performance, as it causes the vibrations of all the harmonics or overtones of the strings to carry throughout the concert hall, and *Eusebius* is the intensely private side of Schumann, whose extrovert nature was given the name of *Florestan*.) The pedal in Chopin is not as ostentatious or as thick as in Schumann, but it is fairly continuous, and is used to emphasize the lines of the contrapuntal structure, the bass in particular, as well as to allow the individual harmonies to reach their full sonority. Moriz Rosenthal, however, who studied with Chopin's pupil Mikuli as well as with Liszt,* insisted that the finale of the Sonata in B-flat Minor, op. 35, must be played with no pedal whatever, and I think that he was right, as any use of the pedal here tends to blur the extremely fast and uniform rhythm of this Presto movement and makes the implied contrapuntal structure of the extraordinary monophonic texture less intelligible (no work shows better how much Chopin learned from Bach, and the single melodic line of this movement that cre-

---

* I could never find out anything about Liszt's teaching methods from Rosenthal, except that it was difficult to persuade Liszt to leave the café and go back to the studio for a lesson.

ates its own harmony is analogous to the works of Bach for solo violin or solo cello). Moriz Rosenthal told me that syncopated pedaling was an invention of the late nineteenth century: that is, not releasing the dampers completely in coordination with the fingers and the striking of the notes, but opening up the sympathetic overtones before and after the attacks. I find this hard to believe, but it is probably true that the most sophisticated uses of the pedal, with half shades and subtle changes, came after the deaths of Schumann and Chopin.

Liszt, together with the so-called school of Liszt formed by the many pupils he influenced, was said to be much more restrained in the use of the pedal, and this can be confirmed by the sober use of the pedal in the recordings of his pupils from the beginning of the twentieth century. It was Liszt who invented so much of modern virtuosity and demanded so much physical power from his interpreters, and composers of the often splendid piano music of the late nineteenth century from Reger to Scriabin added very little to piano technique that could not already be found rooted in the work of Liszt and Chopin. The Etudes of Chopin are, generally speaking, technically more difficult than anything by Liszt (except perhaps the original versions of the Paganini Etudes and the *Transcendental* Etudes, revised and made much easier by the composer after he reached the sobering age of forty). But the power demanded by Chopin must come for the most part from the forearm and fingers, while with Liszt the shoulder and back muscles are brought more directly into play. That is why pianists who are not very tall may have to raise the piano chair half an inch or so in order to realize some of the more spectacular creations of Liszt.

It is evident that each historical change of style brings with it a change in piano technique, often necessitating changes in the position of the hand on the keyboard. Late nineteenth-century composers, however, did not innovate technically within the tradition of pianistic style inherited from Liszt and Chopin, except that in the very different work of Scriabin, Rachmaninov, Albeniz, and Reger, pianists had to learn how to play many more notes in a shorter space of time than ever before, a technique partially derived from the famous transcriptions of Liszt and continued later by Leopold Godowsky. Most concert pianists of the time were expected to be able to make their own arrangements of songs, opera arias, and Strauss waltzes, transcriptions which exploited their individual abilities. This created a style of salon music intended almost exclusively for the concert platform: a formidable technical barrier prevented the amateur from approaching it.

Perhaps the most radically new demands on pianistic technique were made at the beginning of the twentieth century by Debussy. In his work the range of tone color was enlarged, most evidently towards the softer sounds (it is true that Debussy once remarked that he would like to get rid of the initial percussive sound of the hammers on the strings), but there are also passages of extraordinary violence. In the soft sonorities of Debussy the hand must often be placed very close to the keys, so that the note is struck with minimal movement: that allows the note just to "speak" and diminishes the impact of the hammer. The work of Debussy is basically conceived always for public performance in spite of its air of intimacy: that is its special quality. This intimacy is evident throughout his opera *Pelléas et Mélisande,* and it transforms a large theater into a small room. It is with the work of Ravel, however, that the writing for piano almost always gives the effect of being heard at a distance. In his work, the dissonances are hidden in the center of the harmonies as in a cluster. Debussy often places his dissonances in another part of the keyboard away from the principal chord, and this creates the effect of a contrast of registers that reveals the special qualities of the sonorities of the treble, bass, and middle ranges of the piano with a power that no composer had ever achieved or, indeed, tried to achieve, before him.

The greatest masters of early twentieth-century modernism, Schoenberg, Stravinsky, Webern, and Berg, contributed very little to changes in piano technique. For none of these composers was piano music the medium for their finest work, although Stravinsky relied on the piano for the act of composing, and both Schoenberg and Berg used the piano for initial experiments in a new style. Schoenberg's first miniatures are the great set of six pieces, opus 19, the first piece he composed in the new twelve-tone technique is the gavotte from the Suite, op. 25, and the first piece of twelve-tone music he published was the Waltz from the pieces for piano, op. 23. Berg, too, commenced his attempts at the new twelve-tone style with the Chamber Concerto for Piano, Violin and Wind instruments. Schoenberg's way of writing for the piano, however, stems essentially from Brahms, as he himself claimed, although the influence of Debussy is palpable in opus 19. Berg's piano music (essentially the early Piano Sonata, op. 1, and the Chamber Concerto) derives from late nineteenth-century style. Performances of the works of these two composers is often vitiated by the belief that since this is avant-garde music, one must hear all the details all too clearly played. Berg's very fast metronome mark for the first movement of the Chamber Concerto implies a more impressionistic performance in the style of Richard Strauss, who was appalled when his work was rendered with exaggerated clarity ("Gentlemen, you are playing all the notes," he said reprovingly to the Boston Symphony after they had practiced for a week before his arrival in order to impress him with the rapid opening septuplet for the low strings of *Don Juan*).

Stravinsky's piano style was more original in its neoclassical austerity, but added little to piano technique as such. His most important work for the piano is not to be found in the two large solo pieces, the Sonata and the Sérénade, impressive as they are, or even in the Capriccio for piano and orchestra, the Concerto for piano and winds, or the late Movements for piano and orchestra. The passages in his work that exploit the sonorities of the piano with the greatest originality are found in the concerto-like cadenzas for piano in the second scene of *Petrouchka,* and, even more imaginatively, in the spare writing for the four pianos that, with added percussion, make up the entire orchestra for the ballet *Les Noces.* Most striking is the first version of *Le Sacre du Printemps* of Stravinsky, which is for one piano four hands. He always intended to orchestrate it, of course, but the four-hand version astonishingly does not sound like a piano reduction of an orchestral work but like a piano piece in its own right, brilliantly conceived for the two performers. (When he later orchestrated it, he made several changes.) It is, in my opinion, Stravinsky's finest work for piano. This four-hand version is a maverick, as four-hand music was played for the most part privately at home, and rarely in public, and Stravinsky cannot have expected any frequent public presentation of this version, which sounds like a concert piece not intended for household amusement. It is important, however, in demonstrating how little Stravinsky's art depended on his famous craftsmanship of orchestration, and how powerfully the neutral sonority of the piano based so much on pitch alone was still capable of conveying the most important and revolutionary musical conceptions. When he finished the piano version, Stravinsky took it to Debussy, and they read it over together at the piano: at the end Debussy got up and left without a word. I wonder what the sight-reading performance sounded like, and what Debussy actually thought at the time. In any case, in the Etude *pour les agréments* ["for ornaments"], he produced a clear reminiscence of the opening pages of the evocation of the Russian Spring night that opens *Le Sacre.*)

From Debussy's Etude pour les agréments

The young composers of the 1920s and 1930s made no change to the way of playing the piano that had been developed from 1830 to 1850, with the exception of Sergei Prokofiev, who was influenced like most Russians by the French tradition, but who exploited the dry percussive sonorities of the instrument as no one had done before. His most remarkable work seems to me the earliest pieces, above all those that combine the dry attacks with a delicate lyricism; certainly if the invention of a new and original style of pianism is the criterion, his masterpiece is the cycle of twenty miniatures, *Visions Fugitives.* The accomplished work of Hindemith, Copland, Shostakovich and others contributed interesting music to the repertoire but added nothing new to piano technique. Most of the works were small scale: very few piano compositions of the 1920s and 1930s require the large concert grand piano. Smaller instruments would be adequate, and almost no important works exploit the sound of the largest instruments with the exception of the Bartók and Rachmaninov concertos. The solo piano music of Bartók, a great pianist as well as a great composer, is less innovative than his string quartets and the famous Music for Strings, Percussion, Celesta and Piano. His solo works mix the Central European tradition and folk material with the influences of Debussy and Stravinsky. The experiments with clusters and polytonal effects by Charles Ives's music for piano began obscurely to be known during these years, but found real understanding only later. The new ideas in the use of tone color on the piano developed by Olivier Messiaen in the 1930s remained hidden from the general public until the early 1950s. By that time, several composers, John Cage in particular, had experimented with prepared pianos, placing different kinds of material on the strings of the piano to make unusual sounds. These experiments have not survived very well, nor did the novel technique of requiring the pianist to stand up and reach into the piano to strum the strings have much of a future. As I have remarked, it is significant that no purely mechanical attempts to make the sound of a piano more varied and more picturesque have survived except for the soft pedal.

At the end of the 1940s, however, the sonatas of Pierre Boulez, Elliott Carter, and Samuel Barber once again called for the sonority of the concert grand piano. Composers began to invent novel contributions to piano technique, principally Pierre Boulez and Karl-Heinz Stockhausen. The compositional ideas of the latter have always seemed to me essentially more stimulating than their actual working-out in sound, but Boulez has an extraordinary ear for sonority, more refined than that of his teacher Messiaen. This sensitivity to sound determines the structure of his work and is intended to shape the performance. On one occasion, when I played *Constellation-Miroir* from the Third Piano Sonata for him to prepare for a recording, he suggested that I make more of a gradual slowing-down of one passage. I observed that he had marked the slowing-down to go from 96 on the metronome to 72, and that I had already reached something like 50. "That makes no difference," he replied; "follow the sonority." The rhythm in his music must often be established not so much by a preestablished scheme, but freely by the performer or conductor in relation to the acoustics of the hall. There are also works of his like the slow movement of the second sonata for piano in which much of the rhythmic effect derives not from the initial attack of the notes but from their release. Boulez was only twenty years old when he wrote this work, but this aspect of it has influenced composers that followed him.*

In general, Boulez envisages much of his work as played with a supple, somewhat fluctuating tempo, a sort of continuous *tempo rubato*. What he takes from Debussy is the importance of register, and that partly accounts for his revolt against the twelve-tone technique as it was practiced by Schoenberg and taught in its most academic version to Boulez by Réné Leibowitz (I have always suspected that Boulez's notorious manifesto *Schoenberg Is Dead* really signified "Kill Leibowitz"). In Schoenberg's Pieces for piano opus 19 and in *Erwartung*, which were atonal but not twelve-tone, the sense of register is explored successfully, but with the arrival of the dodecaphonic system, Schoenberg retreated to a more old-fashioned view in which it was more important for a note to be an E flat, for example, than whether the E flat was a high or low note. To a listener, however, the register of a note is more significant for its sonority than the actual pitch and consequently register plays a preponderant role in Boulez's scores. The use of the pedal is also novel in his piano music, above all in the third sonata where he explored the fact that striking a bass note very loud while holding the pedal down and then immediately changing the pedal several times very fast removes part of the fundamen-

---

* The second sonata is partly a modern realization of academic sonata form (not only does the first movement have an exposition with two sets of themes, a development section and a recapitulation, but there is a scherzo with a trio and an abridged *da capo*). It is also a ferocious parody of the traditional form: Poulenc is said to have called it sardonically The Death of the Sonata.

tal note and successively reveals more and more of the harmonics, as if the pitch gradually rises as the sound is sustained.

Register also plays a more basic role in the music of Elliott Carter, and this gives his harmony greater consistency, making his music more easily intelligible and convincing than the works of some other atonal composers. The systematic use of the twelve-tone system does not automatically bring this conviction: comparing two dodecaphonic composers like Schoenberg and Berg, for example, the consistency of Berg's harmony is more clearly evident than that of Schoenberg, whose genius for the expressive motif was much more evident than his harmonic construction. The use of register by Carter (perhaps the only major composer of his time who has never written a single twelve-tone piece) fosters a different approach to the piano, as it implies that one must pay a much greater attention to articulating dynamic levels in order to bring out the specific quality of the sound of the register and the way it recurs. But the most novel contribution of Carter to piano technique is his use of two simultaneous levels of dynamics in a way that is radically different from the classical distinction between melody and accompaniment. One level of harmonies may move softly and steadily, but almost always rhythmically out of phase with another level, which may be a single forceful line with a continuously changing speech rhythm: the two levels interact but remain absolutely distinct. This develops an abnormally tight convergence and cooperation of tone color and rhythm. Physically the music of Carter requires new piano techniques in his deployment of simultaneous multiple rhythms—or, rather, multiple tempi. It is not difficult to play seven against three—in the Paganini Variations, Brahms asks for four against nine, and then eight against nine—but it can become more difficult, toward the end of Carter's Double Concerto for Harpsichord, Piano and Two Chamber Orchestras, when every fourth note of the septuplets is marked *cantabile espressivo* and every fifth note of the triplets is sustained: in this case, one is obliged to appear not to let the left hand triplets know what the right hand septuplets are doing. Cross accents are one thing, but these cross-tempos require an adjustment in one's bodily response to the rhythm of music which many pianists find hard to achieve.

The acknowledged masters of avant-garde modernism after 1920 have not been able to attain the popularity of the great figures of the eighteenth and nineteenth centuries. Schoenberg, for example, provoked the same resentment that Beethoven and Wagner originally met with, but he has not in the end won general acceptance, as they have. Bartók, Berg, and Webern are not as welcome to the larger public as Donizetti and Brahms. Even Stravinsky does not evoke the same public affection as Verdi. If relatively few pianists will attempt the more imposing works of the piano literature composed after 1920, this is not so much because the public does not favor this music, but because so many of today's professional pianists and certainly the great majority of amateurs are unable to come to terms with it. Most of the distinguished pianists of the 1930s, for example, performed no modernist works. Artur Schnabel composed atonal music, but never played any of the works of his contemporaries. Claudio Arrau was perhaps the only important figure of that earlier generation able to take on an important modernist piece, and I heard an excellent performance by him of Schoenberg's Three Piano Pieces op. 11 broadcast by the BBC once when I was in London. The recent critical reaction against modernism has, however, paradoxically inspired many younger pianists today to take on some of the most ambitious works.

To comprehend the distaste for modernism, it must be admitted at the start that the greatest works of modernism in all the arts are, much of the time, fundamentally disagreeable when first encountered. This dates back to the origins of modernism in the Romantic movement. In the manifesto of Romanticism, the "Fragments" by Friedrich von Schlegel from the *Athenaeum* of 1798, we find:

> *If once you write or read a novel for its psychology, it would be extremely inconsequential and petty to want to avoid even the most boring and most detailed analysis of unnatural lusts, horrible cruelty, shocking infamy, disgusting sensual or spiritual impotence.*

For Schlegel, as for the other German Romantic writers, "the novel" signified not simply the long fictional narrative that we mean today by the term, but the synthesis of literature that could combine elements of poetry and drama. They wished to represent the whole of experience, not merely an idealized and generally agreeable selection from it, and to show it with all its complexity. Composers and performers, too, wished to enlarge the experience of music. Not only did the works of Mozart and Beethoven and of the generations that followed offend many contemporary listeners, but the playing of Paganini was a shock to the original audiences, as they had never heard a violinist attack his instrument with such ferocity and make such horrid noises with it. The brutal sonorities of some of the early works of Liszt inspired by the playing of Paganini were equally disconcerting at first.

It took some time from 1798 to carry out Schlegel's radical program for modern literature, but, starting at least with Flaubert, it has been achieved with magnificent success over the years. *Madame Bovary* was found scandalously disgusting by many contemporaries, and *L'Education Sentimentale* was even more shocking in the deliberate choice of a hero who was undistinguished and so uninteresting as to be almost contemptible. Not many lovers of literature have been able to get all the way through Joyce's *Ulysses,* and I have met only two people who have read every word of *Finnegans Wake.* Recent claims that Joyce was elitist because *Ulysses* was published in an expensive and limited original edition are absurd: the publishers judged correctly that the initial sale would not be large, and hoped to be able to recoup the expense of printing. There is no reason to think that Joyce and his publisher, Sylvia Beach of Shakespeare & Co., would not have been delighted if it became a best-seller (which eventually happened, largely due to the scandal of its censorship). Similarly, Anton von Webern said that he hoped the day would come when the postman would deliver his mail whistling a twelve-tone row. Every avant-garde artist would welcome popularity provided it was given to the art that it pleased the artist to produce. (Painters have been less burdened by the foolish accusation of elitism, perhaps because the enemies of modernism tend to be impressed or intimidated by the enormous sums paid for the works of Picasso, Matisse, Jackson Pollock, de Kooning, Jasper Johns, and others.) Modernism in painting and literature is more easily supported than in music, as one can walk by the painting rapidly or put the book down. But sitting patiently through a public performance of a long modern work of music is torture to the unsympathetic listener, and it is not surprising that it occasionally inspires disruptive exits calculated to spoil the pleasure of those who remain.

Few people would deny that parts of *A la Recherche du Temps Perdu* are extremely tiresome, even those lovers of Proust who judge the work a masterpiece, or that the operas of Berg—*Wozzeck* and *Lulu*—represent sordid and depressing subjects unredeemed by heroism, nobility, or even decency, and with the profoundly cynical realism magnified by the music. Many of the most admirable modern poets, starting with the great figure of Mallarmé, and continuing with Rilke, Wallace Stevens, and Paul Celan, are incomprehensible even to a large majority of college graduates. The list of glorious works of modern literature that are considered for perfectly good reasons disgusting, boring, or unintelligible is very long, and I by no means intend to attack their exalted status by pointing this out. Disgust, bewilderment, and even the most exasperated irritation are not insurmountable barriers to aesthetic appreciation; they may in fact be a stimulus. It would not be quite true to say that the greater a work of modernist art is, the more repellent it will seem to be at our first contact with it, but it may often appear to be so to those who reject the style. Furthermore, the masterpieces of modernism can still today seem to be incompetent. Even after Delacroix's death when he was almost universally acknowledged to be one of the national glories of French art, his most radical drawings were characterized by the Minister of Fine Arts as the scribbling of a child. The great modernist paintings from Picasso to Jean Dubuffet and the New York School may appear to the average man of good sense like the work of children, savages, or perverts whose purpose is to distort and insult reality.

These adverse reactions have not lacked sympathy or understanding within the avant-garde itself. In 1938 Schoenberg fled

Germany to Barcelona; during the year he lived there, the International Society of Contemporary Music scheduled a festival concert there and Webern wished to conduct Schoenberg's *Music for a Film Sequence.* Schoenberg refused permission. He had made many friends in Barcelona, and played tennis with them, and what would they think of him, he said, when they heard that horrible music?

Nevertheless, modernism has engaged the passionate loyalty of a minority, and if the passion is not full compensation for the failure to gain general approval, it is still a guarantee that the music will continue to be performed. It is not, I think, sufficiently recognized to what an extent taste is a matter of will power. I am told that when I was a five-year-old child whose experience of music was largely confined to Beethoven and Wagner, my first reaction at hearing Debussy was to insist that there should be a law prohibiting such works. To appreciate a new and difficult style, as I have said, takes an act of will, a decision to experience it again. That is why Rimsky-Korsakov wisely told his young pupil Stravinsky not to listen to Debussy, as he might get to like it.

A love of classical music is only partially a natural response to hearing the works performed, it also must come about by a decision to listen carefully, to pay close attention, a decision inevitably motivated by the cultural and social prestige of the art. Of course, it is true that not every taste developed in this way will become permanent. The music of composer Johann

Adolf Hasse (1699–1783), once one of the glories of the 1700s, and perhaps the most famous living composer of the 1760s, rapidly disappeared by the end of the eighteenth century, probably forever except for curious historians of music, while the more obscure J. S. Bach became more famous with each successive decade. The fervor inspired by Schoenberg has already lasted longer than the ephemeral glory of Hasse. The reaction of distaste, incomprehension, and even disgust inspired at first by Beethoven and Wagner altered with time through the pressure of professional musicians and with successive rehearings of the works, into an obsessive admiration, even into an addiction. For a smaller number, the works of the great figures of the twentieth-century avant-garde are equally addictive. As long as this addiction continues to be found among musicians, the music will survive. Music that we want to play is assured of a future.

There is no question that a taste for difficult contemporary music is acquired with less ease than a taste for Romantic opera. It takes more effort, more willpower, to arrive at an understanding of its language. The first time I played any twelve-tone music was in 1952, three short pieces of Milton Babbitt for which I had only five days to prepare in Paris before performing them on a brief tour of Switzerland (the pianist who should have gone on the tour had been taken ill). I practiced the first piece, which lasts about three minutes, for four hours on the first day. The next morning when I returned to the piano, it was as if I had never seen the piece. I was in despair, full of self-doubt and even panic. The third day it clicked, and I learned the two other pieces rapidly. I had, without quite knowing how—certainly not by analysis—learned the language. It has become a little easier for music lovers to absorb the atonal style as we have heard it so often over the years in film scores, where it generally represents an approaching menace, and the familiarity has seeped into the public unconscious. When I was in college in the late 1940s, there was only one singer, the soprano Bethany Beardsley, who could negotiate the pitches of the songs of Webern. Today any of the graduates of the vocal department of Juilliard can sing them with ease if not always with inspiration. Many musicians are disinclined to approach the more difficult style of the twentieth century. They are missing an intense pleasure. In all the arts a difficulty overcome has a savor that the blandness of the more facile experience will never provide, and it is the difficult works of the past century that are the most likely to descend to posterity.

A distaste for modernism is understandable and needs neither defense nor apology. It is not an easy style to come to terms with; and it requires, as I have said, a determined act of will. But in the end it is simpler to succeed in loving the music of Alban Berg than to read *Finnegans Wake*. What deserves only dismissal, nevertheless, is the critic who, aping the naive child in the fairy tale who claimed that the emperor has no clothes, maintains that we who love the difficult masterpieces of our time are only pretending, lost in admiration before something which does not in fact exist. Our society has an absurd tolerance for obscurantists who wish to deny the relevance of the art and science they do not understand. The more obtuse critics of modernism, treated seriously by some journalists, are like the creationists (also treated seriously by many journalists and even senators) who attack evolutionary theory because they think Darwin said that we are all descended from monkeys. The message of both groups is a simple celebration of ignorance: what I do not understand is not worth understanding. They may deserve our sympathy, but in the end there is no reason to listen to them.

POSTLUDE

THE TRADITIONAL CONFIGURATION of the key-board—its arrangement of black and white keys—has had a largely unrecognized influence on the history of harmony, because of most composers' dependence on the piano for inspiration—an influence that may perhaps not be considered completely benign. The keyboard as it is constituted was perhaps best fitted for music from 1700 to 1880 and has become more and more awkward since then. By the late eighteenth century music was relying heavily on the transposition of motifs, or even whole sections of a piece, from one tonality to another. Playing a melody in C major feels very different under the hand from playing it in F-sharp major. We are physically in a different realm. Most musical works of the late 1700s begin in tonalities using mainly white keys: as the work progresses more and more black keys are used and the hand begins to take different positions in order to realize the same phrases. This means that the central section of most large works, where important and distant modulations occur, is not only different from the opening bars, to the ear and to the mind, but also the performer's sense of touch perceives the alterations and alienations of the original melodic forms. In the development section of the first movement of Mozart's Concerto for Piano in B-flat Major, K. 595, for example, the main theme appears in the spectacular and radical series of B minor, C major, C minor, E-flat major, E-flat minor, ending in the conventional goal for a classical development, the relative minor, G minor. Each playing is a different physical experience for the hand, with different fingering, and we may say that the harmonic structure with its dramatic tension is immediately and directly perceived by the tendons and the muscles of the performer. This represents the golden classical age of Western piano music, when conception, hearing, and touch all cooperate. The synthesis of tactile, aural, and intellectual experience would be difficult to repeat.

Equal temperament was first used on keyboard instruments, and it swept throughout the whole field of music, vocal as well as instrumental. It is sometimes said that Bach did not use fully equal temperament but some compromise between equal and natural tuning. However, he transposed his French overture from C minor to B minor (apparently, as Hans Bischoff suggested, to add an H to the keys of *A B C D E F G* in the first two books of his *Keyboard Exercises*—the note B is H in German and the German B is our B flat). In any tuning other than equal temperament no two tonalities are farther apart in harmonic character than C minor and B minor, so either Bach was using equal temperament or he did not much care what the tuning did to his compositions (perhaps B minor sounded agreeably odd and exotic)—in any case, the different tunings had little effect on his procedures of composition. Even in his string quartets, Beethoven also implied a system of equal temperament, although the string players certainly adjusted their pitches for expressive reasons, and still do so. He was capable of writing A sharp for the cello at the same moment that the violin plays B flat. Theoretically, the equal temperament imposed by the keyboard instruments reigned supreme.

In the end, equal temperament may be said to have destroyed one of the basic elements of classical eighteenth-century triadic tonality—the distinction between modulation in the dominant or sharp direction and modulation in the flat or subdominant direction. Modulating in the flat direction brings us from the basic C major, for example, eventually to G flat major, and modulating in the sharp direction brings us to F sharp major: in natural tuning, these two keys are different, but they are the same in equal temperament.* What happened in the long run is that equal temperament obliterated the sense

---

* Going around the circle of fifths in the subdominant direction, one descends all the fifths C, F, B flat, E flat, A flat, D flat, G flat. In the dominant direction, one rises C, G, D, A, E, B, F sharp. The dominant direction is the more basic, which is why all the notes starting from C are white keys on the piano until F sharp. The subdominant is related to the chromatic alterations of the minor mode, and after C and F all the descending notes are on black keys.

of the direction of modulation. This sense was always present as an important component of the classical musical system from 1700 to 1800, and it was scrupulously preserved by Beethoven: the dominant was a source of drama, of raised tension, the subdominant a resolving force and a potential source of lyricism. The distinction was already lost for Schumann and irrelevant to Chopin, and an increasing chromaticism based on equal temperament finally drove it out, in spite of Brahms's successful reconstruction of some part of the classical procedure. The symmetrical complexity of a style that opposed diatonic and chromatic harmony was being eroded by the piano.

It can be taken as symbolic that in the basic key of C major on the piano, the diatonic notes are a pure, chaste white, the chromatic notes a more sinister black. After 1825, for more than a half century, a complex network based on mediant relationships,* which are basically chromatic, and on the equally chromatic contrast of major and minor modes was an effective substitute for the more clearly defined classical system. With Verdi and Wagner, the tonal synthesis of an entire long work is no longer attempted, but the unity of long sections of their operas is still clearly realized (and in *Meistersinger* and *Parsifal* one may even speak of a harmonic plan for the entire opera).

---

* A mediant relationship is a modulation by a third (going, for example, from C major to E major or to A-flat major). This was already important to Beethoven who, however, always preserved a classical preparation for the new key through its dominant. This preparation was largely dispensed with by Chopin and Wagner and by the generations that followed.

Modern so-called neotonal music, however, inspired by a natural reaction to the complexities of modernism, is only a hollow simulacrum of either the eighteenth- or nineteenth-century systems. In today's neotonal works, the hierarchical richness and complexity of the eighteenth-century structures have completely disappeared; even the major-minor contrasts of nineteenth-century style have lost their capacity for controlling the large-scale form. Each single phrase may be tonal in today's new conservative movement, but the tonal structure of an entire piece is either abandoned or given a simplistic form which does not recognize the emotional intensity of full triadic tonality. That system required an intensity of listening that most of us are perhaps no longer willing to provide. In Mozart, every harmony is related to the central key, and has a different harmonic significance according to its distance from the center, and the meaning of each chord also depends on whether the harmony was reached from the sharp or the flat direction. This was an extraordinarily grand expressive style that depended on a complex hierarchy that has disappeared forever. We can learn to appreciate it, but continuing to compose with this system is as artificial and, in the end, as impossible as trying to write poetry in the language and style of Chaucer or Shakespeare. Neotonal music is a poor substitute for the subtle and powerful work of the past. It is true that Schoenberg once said uneasily that there was a great deal of good music still to be written in C major, but nobody has succeeded in writing any of it, and it is unlikely that anyone ever will—unless, like our neotonal composers today, we think of C major as something loosely organized, much more primitive, less richly concentrated and, in fact, more naive than the C major of the era from Bach to Chopin.

The piano, hero and villain, which helped to confirm the full hierarchical system of tonality in the late eighteenth century and was also one of the forces that conspired to destroy authentic classical tonality chromatically from 1830 to the first decades of the twentieth, may itself be becoming obsolete. No longer does every lower middle-class household have a piano, on which the children can pick out tunes and discover a vocation for music. Mechanical devices for producing music have taken precedence over playing at home. For the amateur musician, the more convenient guitar has replaced the piano as the preferred instrument. Fifty years ago the piano was still the great vehicle not only for the classical tradition but also for jazz. Perhaps because it is too unwieldy to be easily portable, or because of the high wages demanded by stevedores today, the piano has not won an important role in rock or rap.

I do not know if new ways of using the piano will be found in the future. I do not know if the institution of the piano recital will survive. Nor do I know if the general public will continue to listen to pianists on records, nor whether some families will still buy the embarrassingly cumbersome pieces of furniture that grand pianos have become in our apartments.

Music, a basic human need, will of course survive, but whether the piano repertoire in all its variety will go down without interruption to future centuries remains in doubt. I think that these problems, social and economic rather than artistic, will eventually find a solution, but perhaps not one that we can anticipate. However, the survival of the piano repertoire from Bach to Berio will depend essentially not on whether anyone wants to hear it, but on how many will want to play it and refuse to settle for anything else. A fervent passion for performing a work of music or on a musical instrument will always find or create an audience. If there are still pianists in the twenty-second century, there will be a public willing to listen to them, but it is the physical pleasure of playing as well as hearing the piano that holds the key to the future of the music written for it.

ACKNOWLEDGMENTS

This book developed out of an invitation by *The New York Review of Books* to give a lecture at the New York Public Library on spirit and technique in the art of music. The lecture, published in *NYRB* in October 1999, appears in part here, considerably revised.

I am grateful for the advice given me over many years by record producers, above all the late Jane Freedman, Tom Sheperd, Paul Myers, Klaas Posthuma, and, most recently, cogently, and generously, Max Wilcox. All my thanks to the piano technicians who have advised me what to look and listen for in a piano—starting many decades ago in the Steinway basement with Morris Schnapper, who made me feel that I had truly arrived when he asked for a ticket to my recital. Too many friends—pianists, critics, musicologists, and simple civilians—have given me ideas, advice, and help over the years to be listed here, but I should like to thank Robert Silvers of *NYRB* for his stimulus and Bruce Nichols of The Free Press for all his help and encouragement.

INDEX

Index

Index

Haydn, (Franz) Joseph, 8, 26, 42, 44
  Piano Trio in E Major, 54
  works of, 177, 178
Hess, Myra, 92
heterophonic forms, 42
Hoffman, Josef, 2, 108, 191
horizontal dimension of sound, 28, 42
Horowitz, Vladimir, 5, 80, 164–65, 166, 191
  hand position of, 3
  hands of, 2
Humoresk (Schumann), 6
Hungarian Dances (Brahms), 182
Hungarian Rhapsody (Liszt), 5

improvisation, 17–18, 38
Ingres, Jean-Auguste-Dominique, 12n
instrumental music, vocal music and, 9, 17
Intermezzo in A Major, op. 118 no. 2 (Brahms), 9
interpretation, 18, 38, 39, 40, 98, 101–102, 113, 153
Iturbi, José, hand position of, 3
Ives, Charles, 216

Josquin des Prés, 44
Joyce, James, 222

Katchen, Julius, 126n
keyboard
  composing at, 16. *See also* piano, composing at
  configuration of, 229–30
keyboard instruments, 15, 18, 52
keyboard literature
  historical editions of, 177–78
keyboard repertory, 93–94, 95, 96, 97–98, 102, 103, 112–14, 176, 187, 235
  in eighteenth century, 175, 180, 183
  in nineteenth century, 177, 179–80, 183, 202
  private, 175–76, 177, 179–82, 199
  public, 176, 177, 180, 181, 183, 195
  in twentieth century, 181–82

Kirkpatrick, Ralph, 58, 196, 197–98
Kreisler, Fritz, 92

Landowska, Wanda, 196
Le Gray, Gustave, 163
learning music, 41
learning piano
  and history of music, 40, 43–44
  when very young, 90, 92
Leçons (Couperin), 44
"Les Adieux" (Beethoven), 55
Lipatti, Dinu, 1
listening, to oneself play, 33–34, 36, 38
Liszt, Franz, 5, 6, 30, 39, 42, 51, 122n, 135, 181, 186–87, 209n, 222
  harmonics and, 26
  Hungarian Rhapsody, 5
  playing, 210–11
  transcription by, 57
  works of, 177
Liszt, School of, 4, 30, 210
Lisztian octaves, 4
Lulu (Berg), 223

Mahler, Gustav, 44
market for piano music, 8
master class, 100–102
Mazurka in C-sharp Minor (Chopin), 21
melody, 43
memory, 89
  in adults, 90, 91
  in children, 90, 91, 92
  involuntary state of, 37, 40
memory training, 91
Mendelssohn, Felix
  works of, 177, 178
Messiaen, Olivier, 216
Meyer, Gustave, 58
Michelangeli, Arturo Benedetti, 80, 131
microphone fright, 143
mimicry of vocal difficulty, 9
mind/body opposition, 12, 17
Mitropoulos, Dimitri, 91
modernism, 220–21
  critics of, 227–28
  distaste for, 222–24

Index

Index